PRAISE FOR
EVERYTHING CONNECTS

"Management guru, Faisal Hoque, explains how
'mindfulness' can transform your business."

—*FORTUNE*/CNN MONEY

"The focus on mindfulness in *Everything Connects* sets
it apart to traditional, type-A thinking."

—*FAST COMPANY*

"Provides true framework."

—*ENTREPRENEUR*

"One conversation with Faisal Hoque and you understand
why his new book, *Everything Connects,* is powerful."

—CENTER FOR CREATIVE LEADERSHIP

"*Everything Connects* is as much about business as it is about life."

—DR. MARSHALL GOLDSMITH, *New York Times* best-selling author
and the #1 leadership thinker in the world (Thinkers50/HBR)

"By marrying the power of creativity and innovation, there is very
little we can't accomplish. *Everything Connects* shows where and
how this is happening and inspires us to join in this new era."

—PROFESSOR MUHAMMAD YUNUS, Nobel laureate
and founder of Grameen Bank

"Brilliant! *Everything Connects* helps connect the dots in ways
you've never imagined. It's full of powerful and useful ideas
on how to unleash innovation in your organization."

—FRANK SONNENBERG, best-selling author of *Managing with a
Conscience*, former head of marketing for Ernst & Young, and Top
100 Thought Leaders in America according to *TRUST! Magazine*

"If the industrial era was about building, the social era is about connecting. *Everything Connects* is a guide to— and a celebration of—that connecting process."

—**NILOFER MERCHANT**, best-selling author of
11 Rules for Creating Value in the Social Era

"*Everything Connects* shows why sustainable innovation begins with you—yes, you."

—**DR. VIJAY GOVINDARAJAN**, professor, Tuck at Dartmouth, and author of *New York Times* and *Wall Street Journal* best seller *Reverse Innovation*

"*Everything Connects* provides you with a beginner's mind, helping you to see your company free of misleading preconceptions."

—**JASON L. BAPTISTE**, founder of Onswipe
and author of *The Ultralight Startup*

EVERYTHING CONNECTS

CONNECTS

CULTIVATING MINDFULNESS, CREATIVITY,
AND INNOVATION FOR LONG-TERM VALUE

FAISAL HOQUE

WITH DRAKE BAER

AN UPDATED EDITION

FAST
COMPANY
Press

Distributed by Greenleaf Book Group

For ordering information or special discounts for bulk purchases, please contact
Greenleaf Book Group at PO Box 91869, Austin, TX 78709, 512.891.6100.

Design and composition by Greenleaf Book Group and Sheila Parr
Cover design by Greenleaf Book Group and Sheila Parr

Publisher's Cataloging-in-Publication data is available.

Print ISBN: 978-1-63908-020-5

eBook ISBN: 978-1-63908-021-2

Part of the Tree Neutral® program, which offsets the number of trees
consumed in the production and printing of this book by taking proactive
steps, such as planting trees in direct proportion to the number of trees
used: www.treeneutral.com

TreeNeutral

Printed in the United States of America on acid-free paper

22 23 24 25 26 27 28 29   10 9 8 7 6 5 4 3 2 1

Second Edition

Previous edition published by McGraw Hill, 2014 (978-0071830751).

To my family, friends, colleagues, and partners for your love, inspiration, and support

and

To the readers—the dreamers of dreams

I have become my own version of an optimist. If I can't make it through one door, I'll go through another door—or I'll make a door. Something terrific will come no matter how dark the present.
—Rabindranath Tagore

CONTENTS

FOREWORD

INNOVATION IS A HUMAN ENDEAVOR

By Marshall Goldsmith

AS THE WORLD HAS become more globally connected, our personal interconnections have grown exponentially. The speed and pace of our days have greatly increased. In this busier, more connected world, it can be difficult to take the necessary time to reflect on our careers and our lives. While our opportunities and challenges seem to be growing, the time available to reflect on these opportunities and challenges seems to be shrinking.

My professional mission is to help successful leaders achieve positive, lasting behavioral change. Over the years, I have seen how the leadership behaviors that have led to one level of success might not be the same behaviors needed to achieve a higher level of success. In my coaching, all my clients receive confidential, 360-degree feedback. This feedback comes from managers, peers, colleagues, and direct reports. In many cases, my clients also receive feedback from family members and friends. This comprehensive feedback enables us to see the blind spots that inhibit our growth. When leaders have a complete perspective, they can move forward with clarity. Buddha noted that right understanding leads to right action. One word for such a comprehensive view of life is "holistic."

In problem analysis, the holistic approach takes into account the whole system of causes and effects that have an impact on the problem. If the problem were a knot, the holistic problem solver would review each thread's direction and how they all fit together—how the many parts created the puzzling whole. After seeing how the tangling happened, it can be easy to untie the knot; the solution practically suggests itself.

Holistic problem solving helps us systematically review the messy knots in our lives and then create clear, ready-to-implement solutions.

This book helps us find holistic solutions to problems in our organizations and in our lives. To do this, it combines different disciplines.

While there are many books about understanding business and many books about understanding ourselves, few books address both issues at once. In addressing both of these issues, Faisal Hoque and Drake Baer have drawn upon knowledge from many sources, including organizational theory, neuroscience, and management theory, as well as psychology, spirituality, and self-improvement. Their holistic approach illustrates how these different views of the world can be connected.

The approach described in the book was shaped by the authors' backgrounds. Faisal, the entrepreneur, innovator, and elder of the duo, was born in Bangladesh (near Buddha's birthplace) and found himself in the boardrooms of Fortune 100 companies by the time he was twenty-seven. Drake, the journalist, traveler, and younger of the two, was born in Illinois and found himself in Himalayan meditation retreats at twenty-four years old. There's something disparate, united, and exciting about that combo, and their creative tension is found throughout the argument and adventure of the text. Together, they've created a book that's as much about business as it is about life or as much about life as it is about business.

In today's rapidly changing world, leaders are constantly challenged with questions such as these: *How can we keep improving? What can we do that is new and better? How can we innovate?*

Innovation does not happen on a spreadsheet, slide show, or product line. Innovation occurs in the interaction between people. It is a human process. Faisal and Drake believe that the more we can humanize the way we work, the more innovative we become. I agree with their view that the more we understand the mental and emotional causes of innovation and creativity, the more we can untie the knots that stop our progress.

The human process of innovation is not just something that happens between people; it also happens inside people. Part of innovation is self-discovery. Over my years of coaching, I have learned that we cannot have an effective conversation with others if we do not have an effective conversation inside ourselves. By learning how to better frame conversations within ourselves, we can have more grounded conversations with our teams and our world.

To me, the discussion of work-life balance often misses the point. The very phrasing implies that work and life are somehow disconnected. I don't feel this way about my work and my life, and neither do most of the mega-successful people I coach. Faisal and Drake have done a wonderful job of showing that the change we want to see in the world needs to be consistent with the change we see in ourselves.

Progress is something we are all trying to achieve. As we learn in the following pages, progress feeds our engagement, which leads to our best work. What's exciting is that progress isn't something that only exists out there as some feathery ideal but is something we can arrange in our days, starting today. If we understand all the threads that are knotted together in this thing called a job, this thing called a company, this thing called a nonprofit, then with a little luck and a little reorientation, we can make that progress an integrated part of this thing called life.

Marshall Goldsmith is a *New York Times* best-selling author and the No. 1 Leadership Thinker in the World (according to the Thinkers50 Conference sponsored by *Harvard Business Review*).

PROLOGUE

IF YOU WERE TO poke around the shops of Moscow, St. Petersburg, or a Russian neighborhood in your nearest city, you might find a gorgeously carved little metaphor waiting for you on a shelf—the *matryoshka* doll, what might more commonly be called a nesting doll.

Matryoshka Dolls

On first taking in one of these dolls, you'll find a peasant girl or woman in traditional garb, typically wearing a long, flowing dress called a *sarafan*. But that charming figure is more than meets the eye. Should you meet her with your hands, you'll find that she opens up and another doll is inside. Then that doll opens up into another doll, and that one into another, and on and on until you reach the smallest doll (usually a baby), carved from a single piece of wood.

What appeared to be one figure was, in fact, many figures layered inside one another like an onion, with each inner layer containing a smaller doll and each smaller doll supporting the outer layer. While one figure was actually several, it was also, in a way, one.

Organizations are *matryoshka* dolls. What appears to be one solid thing is, in fact, several. One organization is brought about by many people. In the case of a for-profit business, the outermost layer—that charming peasant girl—is the long-term health of the organization. Then, the revenue over time. But there is another layer: the way that society, the customers, users, and other humans interact with the organization and perhaps buy its products. Then, there's another layer within that: the product. And another layer again: the team that built the product. And another layer within that: the culture that brought together the team. And another layer within that: the psychology, the inner life of the founders or leaders of the organization.

Their mental lives inform the culture, which informs the hires, which informs the product, which informs people's interactions with the company, which shapes the brand, which brings in revenue, which allows the company to thrive—or not.

Somewhere along that causality is a movement from the qualitative to the quantitative. The profits are, of course, tangible: they show up in a spreadsheet. But the causes that created those profits are not. There are no analytics—at least that we know of—that completely capture the inner lives of the people who made the profits. That subtle, private life is not something that translates into spreadsheets very well, but it does predict bottom lines, as we'll discover in just a moment.

Why is this the case? We think it has something to do with the era that we are currently in. "Disruption" is a word that is popular in the business world. It's used to describe the action of one company to provide a value—say, a product or service—much cheaper or at a much greater level of quality than the company currently in that space, which is usually called an incumbent. Often, that is thought to be the result of a jump in technology. For example, how the internet catalyzed the rise of Netflix and the fall of Blockbuster in the United States. (Though we'll later explore how it's really the fault of Blockbuster's fixed, unadaptable structure.)

To put it dramatically, this evidences a shift in the priorities of the world. We previously lived in an era in which optimization and its implied rigidity were the only game in town. We now live in a time of creativity, innovation, and sustainability—for these are the skills organizations need to be continually adaptive. In the same way the *matryoshka* baby is hidden within the peasant girl, there are questions hidden within that need for continued adaptability. What kind of psychological practices predict creativity? Which social behaviors predict innovation? Which organizational structures lead to the sustainability of all these things?

The mission of this book is to find out.

INTRODUCTION

RENAMING ROLES

AN ENTREPRENEUR IS A person who takes responsibility for their economic well-being. A leader is a person who takes responsibility for the impact they make on the world. However, that impact, whatever it may be, is made up of a myriad of causes and conditions. The wise leader is forever a student of causality that makes up their endeavor. It's about knowing all those layers of the *matryoshka* doll. If you're trying to create an app that will change people's lives, what are the elements of that change? Which people are you striving to help? How will you test those elements? Who could build such a device or application? What mental state would that person need to build at their best ability?

The questions will keep unspooling, making the *matryoshka* seem infinite. (Maybe it is!) The role of the leader, as we'll discuss at length throughout this book, is to provide alignment. Why? Because alignment allows people to make decisions and act faster, which propels the velocity of an organization, allowing it to get feedback and grow quicker. But what is alignment, and where does it come from? It's about context.

Why were ancient mariners able to sail without modern equipment? They were able to read the stars (without all our modern light pollution). What the stars gave them was context, a signal from which to plan and act. And a clear night, of course, would provide greater resolution for the stars, making the signal stronger and the decision clearer. The leader is also searching for richer and richer constellations, examining the intersections of the enterprise in question. As we will emphasize throughout this book, this is not merely a matter of analysis but also of understanding. If we are trying to get humans to do something together, we need to understand our and their humanity. Such is the nature of holistic business.

THE JOURNEY TO COME

To borrow a line from Phil Libin, the highly quotable CEO of Evernote, we find that humanizing our working lives is a "sufficiently epic quest" to dedicate our lives to.[1] As we'll discuss, that humanization will yield more positive experiences of work, more creativity and innovation within our organizations, and greater interpersonal bonds between the people we work with. And, as the research plays out, it's the best shot we can give ourselves at creating value for the long term—resulting in initial public offerings for startups and diversified financial rewards for mature companies. Over three sections, we will show how being prosocial—that is, oriented toward others rather than yourself—is one of the most pro-business things you can do, and how being holistic and humanistic are key to doing great work.

As these things tend to arrange themselves, this endless (and endlessly rewarding) journey will take place over three acts. In the first, we will address our own mental experiences, our social interactions, and the mindsets we can adopt to orient ourselves to this holistic, long-term view. In the second section, we will explore the structures that lead to long-term innovation, how to act in a manner that promotes mutual flourishing, and, crucially, how a leader can urge us along in this process. In the third section, we'll see how to arrange our lives and our organizations in a way that leads to long-term value creation, surveying the subtle and not-so-subtle arts of idea generation, decision-making, and creating continuous value.

We recognize that this might be a lot of new vocabulary. But don't take our word for it. The things we're about to describe will be familiar to you, though recontextualized. We've made a concerted effort to show how our individual, interpersonal, and organizational working lives all interconnect. By examining these connections, we'll learn new ways to create, innovate, adapt, and lead. That said, we invite you onto this path of meeting work—again.

AUTHOR'S NOTE: 2ND EDITION

QUITE A LOT HAS changed since the first edition of *Everything Connects* was released. That's why this updated version includes a fourth section offering three new chapters inextricably connected to leveraging and thriving in this flickering environment of change. The first chapter summarizes many of the changes we've experienced during that timeframe, from the COVID-19 pandemic to the explosion of remote and alternative work arrangements. In reviewing many of these events, we can see just how much the landscape has shifted and, in turn, how it's essential to reframe the ways in which we approach how we work, play, and live.

The second chapter covers a deeper discussion of a topic that was included in the first release—mindfulness. This practice, which has been lauded by scientists and practitioners alike, focuses on the value of being in the moment and, as a result, stilling much of the internal chatter our minds often produce. Adding to the value of meditation as a component of mindfulness, we'll cover other aspects of mindfulness, including practices and exercises designed to move mindfulness beyond twenty-minute meditation sessions and into minute-by-minute living.

The third chapter covers the topic of resiliency. The ability to be resilient has always been an essential part of people's physical and emotional toolkits, but it's perhaps never been as critical as it is today. With the ongoing ravages of the pandemic, economic changes, and political uncertainty (just to name a few factors), the ability to "bounce back" and carry on in the face of adversity is a particularly important bedrock of the type of self-awareness cited earlier. Viewed in a different light, resiliency isn't merely an advantageous attribute to possess—it's utterly essential, whether you come by it naturally or need to acquire it. (I'll offer several strategies and exercises to bolster your capacity for resiliency.)

Although these "new" topics add further substance to the seminal focus of the first version of *Everything Connects*, they also further the core message of the original edition—that everything has a relationship to everything else, resulting in a powerful synergy. Phrased another way, our choices and actions in one area of our lives have a distinct and recognizable impact on many others.

For example, take the impact of the COVID-19 pandemic. In addition to utterly reinventing many components of our lives, from work to schooling to how we obtain necessary health care, it also imposed—at least for a good portion of the outbreak—a level of isolation and solitude unlike anything many of us have ever experienced. Lockdowns, sheltering in place, and other measures designed to mitigate the spread of the virus forced us all to lead much of our lives with far less in-person human contact for a more extended period of time than most people alive today have known in their lifetimes.

That has led to a well-documented impact on the mental well-being of many. For instance, in just one study on this issue, health policy analytic concern KFF cited a litany of problems ranging from the increasing pervasiveness of anxiety disorders to growing substance abuse. Further, the report notes that it's not a matter of newly reported cases—the isolation of COVID-19 has also exacerbated mental health problems in people who had been dealing with these conditions prior. COVID-19, it seems, impacted people who had not been experiencing such problems while at the same time making those that already existed that much worse.[1]

Ironically, though, the isolation of COVID-19 also offered enormous opportunities for many to embrace and practice the varied components of mindfulness—meditation, as detailed in the original version of this book, but also the application of mindfulness through the activities of everyday life. While some struggled with the extended isolation, others found the solitude an opportune time for a healthy look inward. In a sense, it was a somewhat forced introduction to a remarkably healthy way of living amid the ravages of a worldwide plague.[2]

The same dynamic also exists with regard to resiliency, another new component of this updated version. While the pandemic, as of this writing, continues to challenge the entire planet, it also affords us all a prime opportunity to develop and strengthen both our individual as well as group resiliency. When faced with limited other options, a challenging environment can prove the best teacher possible in terms of grasping and applying the ability to bounce back from setbacks and even tragedy.

These new and broadened topics of discussion further the original focus of *Everything Connects*. They underscore the reality that first, everything is changing at an exponentially faster rate with no signs of slowing down and, further, rather than that change moving us and our world further apart, the precise opposite is taking place. Now more than ever, everything does indeed connect. How we recognize and react to that increasingly connected dynamic will determine what sort of world we live, work, and play in in the future.

Faisal Hoque
January 2022

PART ONE

PART ONe

WHEN, WHO, AND HOW ARE YOU?

WHILE EFFICIENCY IS NOT the opposite of innovation, the structures and behaviors that create them may be opposed.

If you want people to crank out as many widgets as possible in the shortest length of time, you can probably disregard their well-being—until they die of exhaustion—in favor of getting more and more done. However, if you are instead trying to bring something new into the world, you need a whole different set of behaviors. Creativity, by its nature, is an internal process, so we must take into account the processes happening inside people if we wish to have a group be sustainably, reliably creative. The first part of our journey is dedicated to that understanding.

We will begin by laying out the foundation of our argument, taking a close look at exactly what the innovation economy we find ourselves in is and the levers by which companies can navigate it.

In our second chapter, we will survey the mindsets and skill sets that stabilize people in their encounters with the volatility of entrepreneurial life, centering on the twin virtues of authenticity and mindfulness.

In the third chapter, we will look at what it's like to work with people. Since our present problems demand more than one mind, we'll lay out what it means to effectively work together.

In the fourth chapter, we will take a long organizational view. We will consider the nature of value and how a company can produce it continually. This requires a sense of organizational self, an abiding, flexible pragmatism, and a recognition of the interdependencies inherent in any individual business venture—all topics we will delve into.

Without further ado, let's start delving.

CHAPTER 1

UNDERSTANDING WHEN, WHAT, AND WHO WE ARE

"You cannot step twice into the same river."
—Heraclitus[1]

A CLAY CUP SITS in front of you. How does its function change when it is full versus when it is empty? A full cup is useful in that you can drink from it. You can use the resources within it. But what use does an empty cup have? You cannot drink from it, so how can it be useful? Which would the optimist or the pessimist choose? Is it "better" to be half empty or half full?

Or, conversely, what if you wish to add more liquid to the vessel? Would you want it to be empty or full? What is the function of the liquid, then? What is its value?

Take these questions in for a moment. Chew them, taste them, savor them.

Done? Good.

So, what is that cup? According to the old Zen metaphor we're summoning, the vessel is your mind. It can be full or empty, each with its own implications.

Which mind do you want? Which mind do you want your team to have?

If you want to be an expert—which, if you're reading this book, part of you does—you may privilege the full mind. After all, it's rather impressive to know many things, to be a fount of knowledge. However, expertise implies a sort of rigidity. If your cup is full, it cannot accept more water.

As an entrepreneurial society, we've experienced many things and advanced our skills to a high level. However, if we fixate our conception of the world on the systems we build to represent it, we can lose sight of the world. Instead, we just see our ideas about the world. Since we've established that we have all the insight, we don't allow for more to come in.

This is why we need to maintain what Buddhists refer to as a beginner's mind—a certain playful absence of assumptions. As Shunryu Suzuki writes, "In the beginner's mind there are many possibilities, but in the expert's there are few."[2] Since innovation is the product of repeatedly experimenting with possibilities, we're behooved to approach our work in such a way as to give the maximum surface area to possibility.

Beginner's mind is a practice of approaching our experiences empty of assumptions. This is one of the keys and products of mindfulness meditation, which we'll discuss further in the next chapter. Essentially, a beginner's mind is an empty vessel, waiting to be filled up by the raw data of doing commerce and living life. In this way, we become more vulnerable to insight. Since we don't claim to have come to the final answer, we can more readily welcome new ones.

To paraphrase Adam Pisoni, the Yammer CTO who we'll get to know in the second section of this book, we have to assume that everything we think we're right about today will be wrong tomorrow. This demand is a nuanced understanding of the timeless and the timely. Some parts of life are timeless, such as the nature of consciousness and the nature of relationships (this is why ancient wisdom about these fundamentals remains so deeply resonant today). Other, more emergent aspects of life, such as technology, are intensely timely. The phone you carry in your pocket today is markedly different than the one you carried five years ago, and we can assume it will be different than the one you will have five years from now. This is why we can still look to Socrates for insight into teaching as the transference of knowledge, but we probably wouldn't reach out to him to learn about satellite imaging as transference of knowledge. We have our feet in two streams: the timeless and the timely. And as entrepreneurs—that is, people who take full responsibility for their economic and psychological well-being—we need to develop an appreciation for the differences between the two.

We'd sound a little old-fashioned if we wrung our hands at the fact that everything was changing so damned fast. Instead, it's probably healthier to find the proper adaptation to such a volatile environment. We contend that one of the best things we can do is take the empty cup approach. That is, we appreciate how little we can fully know about our present world and how much less we can know about what will come in five years.

There's a word for not knowing: ignorant. While this word usually has a negative connotation—if someone called either of our authors ignorant, we'd leap to defend our fragile intellectual egos—we hold it can be positive. We can be skillfully ignorant by acknowledging that this is a complex, maybe even opaque world we're working in. From that, we can become good at being ignorant. At an individual level, we can become good at acquiring the new skills that will be demanded of us. And at an interpersonal and organizational level, we can surround ourselves with people who shine light onto our various blind spots and treat them in a way that encourages that expansive behavior. Such practices and strategies will be explored throughout this walk we take together.

ON NOT STANDING STILL

Somewhere along the way, we were convinced that stasis was safer than movement. Consistency feels comfortable; volatility is frightening. And so, consciously or not, we attempt to prove ourselves against life's volatility by cultivating robustness in our lives and our organizations. But as Nassim Taleb's *The Black Swan*—and the financial crisis it predicted—has shown us, the most static of systems are, in fact, the most fragile.[3] If we're going to lead our lives—and our organizations—in a way that's actually in agreement with the world, we first have to understand what exactly it is we're agreeing with.

In his 1942 book *Capitalism, Socialism, and Democracy*, the Austrian-American economist Joseph Schumpeter introduced the notion of the innovation economy. He characterized capitalism by its "violent bursts and catastrophes," a process which he colorfully dubbed "creative destruction."[4]

Schumpeter saw the shifts occurring in the world, moving away from rigid standardization toward the fluidity that we know today. He argued that evolving institutions, entrepreneurship, and technological change were at the heart of economic growth. He also said that the incentive to innovate is what makes capitalism the best economic system. We have to agree.

Since organizations and industries are going extinct, many of the unemployed seek jobs that no longer exist. And while not every industry has been disrupted, they all—whether energy, medicine, military, transportation, or entertainment—have been altered by technology. And while we can read for the signs of which paradigm will be the next to be loosened, we cannot know exhaustively.

To top it off, we're living in a global, increasingly interconnected economic and social environment. As we move further into the 21st century, new technologies are changing these fundamental relationships at an ever-accelerating pace. We call these breakthroughs enabling technologies, and their detection is essential to the systemic transformation this book investigates. Their implementation gives us leverage to compete, innovate, and create into the future.

As well, the developing world is becoming more a part of the developed world. Enabled by technology, developing nations are able to transform themselves over the course of years into productive members of the international commercial society. As Vijay Govindarajan notes in *Reverse Innovation*, the inclusion of the global poor into our economic system will be a development of historical significance.[5] Regardless of the locality you find yourself in, neither the competition nor the opportunities of these emerging markets can be ignored. More and more, there is only one connected system on the planet—and it is constantly reemerging.

Creative destruction, as Schumpeter saw it, represents an ongoing shedding of skin within the market. As Thomas K. McCraw characterizes in his superb *Prophet of Innovation*, Schumpeter saw capitalism as a system in which whole products, enterprises, and firms are swept away continuously. Beyond being the coiner of the term "creative destruction," Schumpeter was the first person to talk seriously of business strategy. He says a strategy can only attain its "true significance" in the context of that stormy process. Creative destruction—the replacement of one product with another or one firm with another—is the essential character of capitalism.

And this capitalism that we have is not one solely by calculations of price (and the emphasis on efficacy that motivates) but of sweeping purges of obsolescence. One product replaces another; a worker replaces another; an industry replaces another. Schumpeter described this kind of competition more powerfully: "[It] strikes not at the margins of the profits and the outputs of the existing firms but at their foundations and their very lives."[6] If this sounds terrifying, that's because it is. Entire industries can be swept away. So, then, the elephant in the room: How do we avoid getting swept away?

THE QUALITATIVE IS THE QUANTITATIVE

Something unprecedented happened in the Bay Area of California in the mid-nineties—the first dot-com boom. But within that boom, there was also research into what would make an organization go bust. Called the Stanford Project on Emerging Companies (or SPEC for short), the longitudinal study led by professors James Baron and Michael Hannan documented the employment practices of nearly 200 young Silicon Valley firms and their subsequent performance.[7]

What's intensely interesting about the research from the Silicon Valley of yore is the way that the qualitative, that is, "mushy" things like culture and the way people within an organization relate to each other, can predict the quantitative, such as an organization's chance at reaching an IPO (and being able to continually grow after it). To that end, the authors named five different prevailing personality types for the cultures within organizations, whose perspectives we'll paraphrase below:

- **Star:** We want elite people doing elite work.

- **Commitment:** We want people to be at home where they work and identify strongly with the company. We have emotional ties to the company.

- **Bureaucracy:** We need everything to be documented and approved.

- **Engineering:** We have technical people doing technical work.

- **Autocracy:** We—management—run the company. You work hard; you get paid well.

These personality types had telling performance outcomes, especially around who performed the best in the long term. Most germane to our discussion are the Star and Commitment types. In Star-oriented cultures, employees come on board due to the challenging work made available to them and the ability to work autonomously. In Commitment types, the employees have "emotional or familial" ties to the larger organization and are selected with great care for what you'd call cultural fit. The firms with the Star model were the least likely to go public, but if they did, they'd do the best financially, whereas the Commitment-based companies were 200 percent more likely to have an IPO. The authors note that the Star firms reminded them of Reggie Jackson, the Hall of Fame baseball player who hit 563 home runs—good enough to be 13th all-time in career dingers—but also struck out 2,597 times. In contrast, Commitment companies are like Ted Williams, who had a high on-base percentage and slugging percentage but was less likely to smash a home run.

"The biggest virtue of the commitment model is that when employees are truly invested psychologically in the success and survival of the organization and their coworkers," Baron wrote to us in an email, "then they are less likely to become disengaged, either when there are initial indications of trouble or when they experience huge financial windfalls due to early success."[8]

The two types remind us of the tortoise and the hare. The Star-powered firm can move very quickly, gathering the "best" people to do the "best" work as fast as possible, but may end up floundering. One reason that the authors suggest—and we'll explore later—is that business life, especially startup life, is tumultuous, and so the social system that can best cope with that volatility is one in which the members have the greatest support from one another—the commitment mentality. To use another lens, the Star system is more individualist while the Commitment system is more collectivist, more other-oriented. This is why, as Baron and Hannan note, when the elite work starts to dry up, the elite workers may flee to a more challenging space, while the emotional investments made in the organization in a commitment model will keep people as part of the group.

This knowledge helps us to better see our path. Since these are our own careers and working lives, we want to be more like Ted Williams than Reggie Jackson, more like the tortoise than the hare. We want to be oriented to the long term. Fascinatingly, that long-term orientation—as Baron and Hannan's research suggests—is something that springs from the relationships that comprise an organization. Our work, then, is to find out the qualities of these familial-type ties that predict consistent, long-term performance and then instantiate them. This, too, will be one of the key quests in our journey.

Sustained innovation is composed of a range of behaviors. Creating value for the long term is a holistic endeavor; it requires both analytical and creative talents. High-performance leaders, unlike their more one-dimensional peers, have built a culture that embraces both approaches to thinking, doing, and communicating. This holism finds its way not just in management but in the cultural character of the organization as a whole. What our research found is that enterprises with a focus on long-term value creation share three common principles, comprising the glue that binds people together in productive collaboration.

To begin with, they have converged disciplines, meaning that ideas from one discipline aren't isolated from another—management isn't far removed from technology, for instance. In the same way that rivers and streams converge to form a delta, the disciplines in a sustainably innovative organization form a single entity.

At a more micro level, this entails cross-boundary collaboration, meaning that no enterprise—and no person or element within the enterprise—operates in a vacuum. Every leader, manager, employee, and contractor has latent ideas for latent problems. As we will explore in depth, the more we can include and the more we can connect the people within an organization, the greater we can increase our overall capacity.

Finally, sustainably innovative organizations have sustainably innovative structures. This can take many forms. Just know that the structure of your organization is going to shape the products and services you provide. Like strategies, the structures can be deliberate or emergent. We'll spend a lot of time appreciating these architectures in the second section of the book. The bedrock beneath all of these factors is to understand what you're organizing for—which is largely a question of when.

As the Stanford Project for Emerging Companies' tortoise and hare suggest, a lot of the success or (perhaps especially) failure that organizations bring upon themselves is due to the time they live in. It seems we humans are creatures of the temporal context we live in. When someone says they're going to "live like there's no tomorrow," they're probably about to do something stupid. Chief executives, those monarchs of late capitalism, are no different. As Alfred Rappaport, the scholar and author of *Saving Capitalism from Short-Termism*, has argued, structuring executive incentives to the short term—think yearly bonuses—has a wrenching effect on the long-term health of an organization and of an economy, as is evident by the financial crisis of 2007 to 2009.[9]

This, too, helps us make our path clear. If we want to do well in the long term, we need to be oriented toward the long term. But what does it mean to be working for the long term? What kind of people working in what kind of way can take the individualistic yet collaborative, experimental yet structured path of sustained innovation? This path, we've found, is a personal and collective journey, requiring intra- and interpersonal skills, those that, with practice, we can begin to embody continually. Above all, sustained growth and innovation are a journey, not a destination. A practice as well as a performance. A taking responsibility for one's fate. An embodiment of entrepreneurship.

WHAT IS THE NATURE OF ENTREPRENEURSHIP?

Business literature heaves with definitions for entrepreneurship and leadership. The excess of definitions perhaps speaks to how many contexts these humble words find themselves in. We often speak of entrepreneurship within a tech or startup space, though surely the family running your neighborhood market is also entrepreneurial. And the individuals in the corporate setting practicing intrapreneurship are entrepreneurial as well.

But how is the energy that these people bring from themselves and into the world different than the community organizer building neighborhood bonds or the volunteer catalyzing economic or health care growth abroad? How is this different than the hospital president making thorough revisions of patient care or the artist building relationships with her audience? Though these cases are all different industries with differing ways of life and prioritization of values, the differences lie less in kind and more in context. If we are going to accommodate all of these contexts, we have to define entrepreneurship broadly. So, let us:

Entrepreneurship is taking ownership of one's economic well-being.

In other words, entrepreneurship is about where we place the responsibility for our experience. It's easy to place the responsibility for our economic well-being and professional health upon outside forces, outsourcing our decision-making to the down economy or the stifling corporate culture. While it's hubris to think one has complete control of one's experience, it's martyrdom to think one has none. An entrepreneur, then, is someone deeply engaged in their experience of life—usually in an economic sense, though we find it applies to cases of general good as well—and willing to do the daily work of transforming it. The entrepreneur is idealistic and pragmatic, sensitive of the world they wish to see, and conscious of the world as it is. The entrepreneur's work, then, is in connecting the two.

RECONSIDERING INNOVATION

While forecasted seventy years ago, Schumpeter's ideas regarding innovation have only recently entered into popular conversation, most notably with Clay Christensen's *The Innovator's Dilemma*, published in 1997. Christensen saw how organizations were fixated on the needs that customers expressed rather than seeking out their unspoken, unmet, or future needs. Coupled with the ability to produce goods at rapidly reduced costs, Christensen coined the term "disruption," which now permeates business dialogue. See: cell phones and landlines, Amazon and bookstores, Warby Parker and the eyewear industry, Blockbuster and Netflix. To be an incumbent—or become an incumbent—is to invite disruption.[10]

Again, we need to return to Schumpeter's point about contrasting companies trying to find the lowest cost for a product versus having entire products being put into the dustbin of history. For a recent example, consider Nokia, who was the leader of the cell phone world since the term existed. That is, until smartphones, those handheld computing devices, made the comparatively "dumb" phone that preceded it intensely obsolete (at least in the developed world). While finding efficiency in the products and processes that we have is indeed important to the work we do, we cannot allow it to blind us to the more mysterious, more existential endeavor of finding what could be the next step forward—or sideways—that could allow an organization to flourish or perish.

We cannot shrink our way to success.

As we define it, innovation is not a single moment, a catharsis, upheaval, or revamping. It is not a change or a one-hit product. Instead, it is a continuous process. If we are going to continually innovate, we need to set up a system that can continually discover. The popular imagination suggests a lonely innovator with a behemoth intellect receiving brief, isolated flashes of insight. This might happen once in a while, but innovation is best when made casual, when it's a product of gathering the best talent, working together in the best way, in an organizational structure most conducive to individual and collective flourishing. Then, the revenue will follow. By systematizing the process, innovation becomes a regular, rather than heroic, occurrence.

Those are the topics of the next two chapters. Before we get there, we must make a further inquiry into the nature of innovation.

TO CURE YOUR BLIND SPOTS, RECONSIDER EVERYTHING

The economic world is an interconnected cacophony. Schumpeter's explosions can happen anywhere, and no matter where the node lies—person within organization, organization within country, country within world—the individual burst affects the whole network. And because that creative destruction could happen anywhere, we must look everywhere.

But we need not be violent. Like a child, we can ask the world how it got there.

We need to question and rethink each thing we do and every institution we have, whether social, governmental, business, education, or health care. We must consistently ask "why?" of the fundamental aspects of our worldview—what is a business for? What is an organization for? Why do we use GDP as a measure of a nation's productivity? Why determine the strength of the economy solely on what consumers buy? Why are some companies one-hit wonders? How do others continue to find success? What comprises innovation? What's the nature of creativity? And what are the causes of all this change?

Why all the reconsideration? Because companies ossify. Bureaucracy and inertia set in, creating "can-I-do-that?" overhead (e.g., inefficiency and costs, to name a few), for every time someone wants to make a decision. As well, a culture of "that's the way things are done here" can begin to set in, stymieing creative discussion and preventing connections with the ultimate arbiters of a company's success: the customer. Even the most traditional of industries need to take these deep looks into themselves.

The Mayo Clinic's Bottom-Up Innovation

Since its foundation in 1889, the Mayo Clinic of Rochester, Minnesota, has been an innovator in health care. The center that W. W. Mayo built was one of the first to incorporate integrated medical care (in what, looking back, was a massive de-siloing) by putting specialists into the same building and allowing them to combine perspectives for evaluations and coordinate their treatment.

In 2002, the clinic reached out to innovation consultancy IDEO to reimagine patient services. The result was their SPARC (See-Plan-Act-Refine-Communicate) Lab launched in 2004, which *Fast Company* writer Chuck Salter describes as a "clinical innovation lab that operates like a design shop." Doctors, nurses, and others act like designers, focusing in on the user experience and prototyping solutions to pain points. By taking this design thinking strategy, the Mayo Clinic is investigating the basis of their industry, the way a patient experiences treatment. This is exactly the kind of bottom-up inquiry that a transformative organization needs to continually make.[11]

ENABLING TECHNOLOGY: THE GAME CHANGER

To painter-illustrator-entrepreneur-activist Molly Crabapple, the whole starving artist thing is a "bulimic response to capitalism." For her, if you want to work within the world of power—and the art world is certainly one brokered by the powerful—you need to be fluent in the language of power, to have a "consciousness of power." You need to be a seeker of opportunities and a builder of relationships so that, as you grow, you can circumvent those gatekeepers.[12]

At the time of interviewing, Crabapple was twenty-nine years old. She makes six figures a year as a full-time artist, as she has for the past three years. This runs exactly opposite to the "lie" that she says gets told to people about the ennobling effects of poverty, the aesthetic virtue found in just scraping by. To be an artist, as her career evidences, you have to also be an entrepreneur.

This is a lesson that was ground into her when she was young, born in Queens, New York, to a political science professor father and an illustrator mother. She remembers being seven years old and sitting with her dad at their kitchen table as he explained to her the nature of capital. She also remembers seeing her mom cultivate her talent and make sacrifices with an implicit trust that financial success would follow, though it never did. Crabapple, in her sweetly acerbic, raven-haired glory, is the fulfillment of both their legacies. She is the skill-cultivating popular artist, as her mother would be, but that idealism is tempered by her father's grounded pragmatism, a commitment to understanding the way the world really works and acting accordingly.

"The creative disciplines are so fame-driven," she said to us. "The reason that people get big book advances is not because they are shining literary lights. It's because their book is going to sell and make money back for the publisher. It's not even necessarily wrong. That's just how it is."[13]

Accordingly, one might rightly consider Crabapple to be the model of the networked artist. She has a razor-sharp understanding of the way that connections create value—a theme throughout this book—and has strived to constantly be growing them.

Her entrepreneurial ventures started with Dr. Sketchy's Anti-Art School, a drawing club that quickly sprouted up chapters in South America, Europe, and Australia. It didn't make any money, she confides, but it did give her a global platform. How strange it is to be a mid-twenties artist being flown to Finland to talk about sketchbooks.

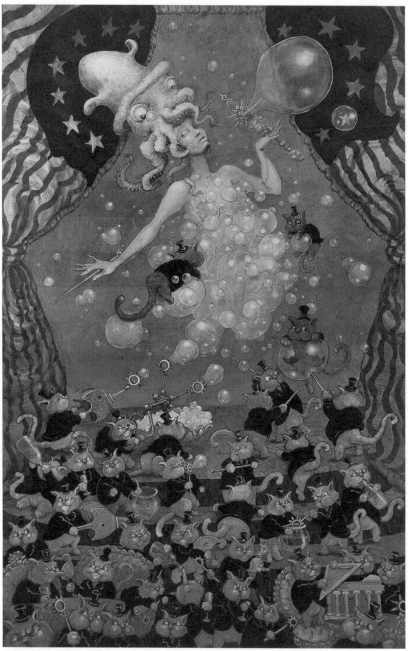

"Great American Bubble Machine" by Molly Crabapple.
Courtesy of Molly Crabapple.

That knowledge of her "platform"—that is, the depth and breadth of her audience—is what's catalyzed her ability to sidestep the gallery gatekeepers. The *New York Times* reported on a drawing-and-burlesque show she put on to reward her fans for getting her up to 4,000 Twitter followers. Now she's at more than 138,600.

That wealth of connections has allowed her to become a force in crowdsourcing. The Kickstarter campaign for *Shell Game* (her love letter to the cacophonous changes of 2011 as epic-scale painting show) earned $64,000 in funding, more than doubling her $30,000 goal. The campaign before that earned $25,000 in funding, eclipsing its $4,500 goal.

But her networked business aplomb doesn't end there. She also monetizes via Etsy (www.etsy.com), the handmade goods network. At the time of our speaking, she had made $20,000 in the past year through print sales there. She's constantly looking to find new ways to repurpose her work by selling prints, licensing reprints to publications, or to be iPhone covers.

In this way, Crabapple is a perfect example of an entrepreneur—a person that has taken full responsibility for her well-being in a financial sense, the way she wishes to live her life, and the impact that she wishes to make upon the world. But to do that, she had to reject the received wisdom that every good artist must be starving and the established structure as the only possible path. "[The big galleries] just want you to repeat the same piece of work that sold well last time until you die," she said. What enabled her independence was an insight into the way technology accelerated connections. The crowd she built online has sourced her artistic projects. Her patron is the people. Or, in classical business-ese, her boss is the user.

Historians talk about technological determinism. Civilizations are marked by their standard of technology, be it stone, bronze, or information. Technology pushes society forward. To an optimist, that's progress. While these advances were unpredictable beforehand, we tell ourselves we knew it all along afterward, reassuring ourselves with our narratives.

Thankfully, we're getting better at constructing the narrative before it happens. We have more powerful abilities to simulate, predict, and identify these changes. We are better able to model enabling technologies, though we'll get to that in the third part of the book. The key, then, is to detect, if not create, these enabling technologies ourselves while they're still embryonic and then heed their call to action.

While we are very clearly awash in enabling technologies at present, we must be vigilantly sensitive to enabling technologies as they appear. For their consequences are wide-reaching, from the collective to the individual level. Recent history shows us why.

While invented in the US, China is the world's largest photovoltaic cell producer, manufacturing over twenty-three percent of global supplies. While consuming unprecedented levels of fossil fuels, China is also poised to become a leader in sustainable power, as it plans to increase its use of solar power fivefold by 2020 (we will see if they hold to this initiative). The implications of becoming a clean-energy-producing superpower are unknown, though we can trust they will be tremendous. But it is not only nations that can leverage enabling technologies. Entrepreneurs of all kinds do as well.

After being rejected by a range of publishers, twenty-nine-year-old Amanda Hocking self-published her novels and promoted them with Facebook, Twitter, and blogs. After two years of diligent promotion from her living room, she earned $2 million. In January 2011 alone, she sold more than $400,000 worth of e-books through Amazon and Barnes & Noble. Her success caught the eye of publishers, and soon St. Martin's Press awarded her a $2 million advance and a four-book contract. While building her social media presence was hard work, it proved to be a transformative factor, allowing her to become the writer she always wanted to be.

That same January of 2011, a revolution was afoot in Cairo, enabled in a similar way. Social media allowed the rapid communication needed to bring 50,000 protestors together in the Egyptian capital's Tahrir Square to demand that President Hosni Mubarak step down. Though the government disabled cell towers and attempted to block Twitter, by Friday, February 11th, over a million people had gathered. Mubarak stepped down; the Arab Spring bloomed.

While dramatically different from one another, each case shows the shared thread of enabling technologies on the role of industries (as the e-book and social media have changed publishing) or countries (as Twitter helped spur on revolution in Northern Africa). In this way, a single enabling technology can take root and shape multiple ecosystems. This is because technology can affect a range of people.

Technology has a way of refracting people's wants. As demonstrated by the above, Twitter provides a telling case study. Co-founder Jack Dorsey grew up in St. Louis, listening to the emergency dispatch center. He noticed that people were always talking in short bursts of sound, micro-sized bits of speech. (Communication, we can agree, is one of the fundamental human wants.) As he told Lara Logan of *60 Minutes*, he noticed that "[People are] always talking about where they're going, what they're doing, and where they currently are."[14] This is where the idea for Twitter came from. He recognized something that people wanted—the ability to communicate quickly with short bursts of speech—and this was enabled by the rise of cell phones and text messages.

Soon we became the center of the dispatch.

TAKEAWAYS

Yes, the world is flat. More importantly, the world is in flux. The creative explosions that Schumpeter spoke of seventy-some years ago are now occurring all over the world, with greater and greater frequency. The startup scene has become a cult of disruption, and that is radiating out into enterprise as well. We live in an unpredictable, unwieldy era. The better we understand this environment, the better we can adjust to it, and the more likely we can flourish.

By uniting opposites, a company can thrive in flux. It is possible for organizations to thrive in the innovation economy, but to do so requires the union of serendipity and process, conceptual understanding and emotional intelligence, theory and practice. In so doing, a company can cultivate perpetual transformation.

The leader acts as catalyst. By instilling processes, eschewing slogans, and gaining buy-in from the team, a leader can take the staid inertia of an organization and tip it toward momentum. To do so requires not only an understanding of the nature of a given industry and ecosystem but also the way people work as a group and individually.

CHAPTER 2

MINDFUL EXPERIENCE, AUTHENTIC SELF

"Everybody needs a passion. That's what keeps life interesting. If you live without passion, you can go through life without leaving any footprints."
—*Betty White*[1]

THE WORDS WE USE to describe best practices tend to take the long view: sustainable, ongoing, continual. And while it's true that the best businesses grow over months, years, and decades, we can only interact with that trajectory in a given day, or more precisely, in a given moment. Taking those two factors into account, the path we've chosen feels daunting. Whether you're talking personally or professionally, we're responsible for our long-term growth in each short-term situation.

What we need is to skillfully and fully engage with both of these timelines. We need to have a long-term orientation and have it made manifest every day. This is the work of instantiating a philosophy, the rigorous, practical, daily work of embodying the changes we want to see in the world. What this demands is to have a two-pronged approach to engaging with our own lives. This demands clarity of goals and clarity of action. Both are born of mindfulness. Both are born of authenticity.

Setting our minds to this is the goal of this chapter. A navigational analogy is useful. Wayfinding comes in two parts: there's knowing the destination which you seek, then there's the step-by-step of arriving there. We want to get clear on the purpose of our work, then find ways to turn that purpose into daily practices. Move the long view into our present view. Take the macro to the micro.

Let's begin with the micro.

THE NEED FOR BETTER TOOLS

As we have discussed, one of the privileges and responsibilities of living an entrepreneurial life is that we can have agency in the world we experience. However, as we nourish our potential—which comes from the Latin for "powerful"—we may work ourselves into situations that require greater tools than the skill sets we received from school or from culture at large. But this shift is not in the sense of what an app or a consultant can give you. What we're talking about is how to manage our own minds amid the constant downpour of messages, the influx of meetings, and the myriad of demands that flood our working lives. We need to find better methods for managing the experiences we've invited into our lives. We might, as Paul Slakey would say, need tools.

Paul, now LinkedIn's director of global solutions and services, had an all-American upbringing. Born in Oakland, California; oldest of six kids; played baseball; had a newspaper route. He studied mechanical engineering as an undergraduate at Berkeley, then worked for IBM and later HP as an engineer, completing awesome projects like designing robots and automated machines. And though he liked being a techie, he realized that his calling was to be a leader. So, he went to the Tuck School of Business at Dartmouth to ease his transition into management. There, he met Warren Buffett, former P&G CEO John Pepper, and former Disney CEO Michael Eisner. "They inspired me to think big," he said to us in an interview.

Soon after, Paul found himself in rarefied air. By thirty-four, he was living near Los Angeles and married with kids. He was working for McKinsey and Co., the highly esteemed consultancy. We'll allow him to describe the situation:

"The premium consulting firm typically consults either for CEO or really senior folks in an organization and charges high fees. The expectation is that you're going to deliver a lot of value if you're going to charge so much. You tend to go in to the client and very quickly put together a hypothesis, and then they expect you to deliver this insight. That leads to ten-hour, eleven-hour, sometimes twelve-hour days. It's interesting and exhilarating but stressful at the same time.

"I was also commuting an hour at a time. I was living south of Los Angeles, but McKinsey's office was an hour away in the city. I was fighting traffic on L.A. freeways every day. I was living the good life, but I was getting more and more stressed. It just hit me; there's got to be more to life than this."[2]

As these things tend to happen, a book found its way to him: *Wherever You Go, There You Are*, with an introduction to mindfulness meditation by the meditator, educator, and physician Jon Kabat-Zinn. And so, Paul began to sit.

"I didn't really know what I was doing, but I would just sit down in my backyard with my hands folded, close my eyes, and try to just breathe and do something besides worry," he recalls. "That was the beginning."

But that soon ended. Paul feared that if he started sitting too much, he would lose his edge. Maybe he'd start to question what he was doing in the rat race.

"Maybe I ought to come back to this meditation stuff after I've got another ten or twenty years in my career under my belt and I've made some money," he remembers thinking. "What happens if I completely lose my desire to work? That's not going to be good."

He stopped meditating in 2000. His career at the time was going great. He was working as a venture capitalist during the dot-com boom, and he soon became CEO of one of his portfolio companies, called Flypaper. But then September 11th, 2001, came, after which Paul recalls money became scarce in Silicon Valley, so they sold the company. While he thought he could hop to another leadership position, the slowdown left a lack of such gigs.

"I went from Paul Slakey, CEO, to Paul Slakey, unemployed!" he wrote to us. "In retrospect, this turned out to be a very pivotal time in my life. I realized that I had become far too attached to my professional identity. Without the title of CEO, I didn't know who I was anymore."

Paul discovered that his happiness and self-worth had become tied to professional success. With a sudden influx of time on his hands, he began going for long runs, writing in his journal, and starting to meditate once again.

"These challenging circumstances created the perfect opportunity for me to test the effectiveness of meditation," he continued. "Gradually, I developed a deep sense of calm power that was not dependent on my external success. I came to see that my job was just a role that I was playing, an important role, of course, but not what defined who I am. My career started to take off again in 2004 and has continued to flourish since then. But now my happiness and identity feel much less dependent on that success, and my meditation practice helps me to keep that big-picture perspective."

Paul returned to meditation for the same reasons he originally found it: to not always feel so wound up or be so much in his head and to have tools to quiet his mind. Contrary to his initial worry, the mindfulness practice informed and enriched his work. This was a counterintuitive truth he saw modeled in the late Thich Nhat Hanh, the noted Vietnamese monk who spoke at Google in 2011. Hanh, whom Martin Luther King nominated for the Nobel Peace Prize in 1967, wrote more than 150 books and traveled the world as a speaker. He was intensely vigorous until his recent passing at ninety-five years of age. Paul saw in him a model to answer to his earlier fear, that, yes, you could be peaceful and engaged.

This understanding is now present in his working life, in the sense of purpose he feels, in the way he can emotionally relate to people, and in how he can buoy himself throughout the day.

"When things come up that are challenges or might be stressful, if I've meditated that morning, it creates that little gap, that little space where I can pause before I react," he says. "Then I can react in a more powerful, constructive way. Life always has challenges, especially if you have a position of responsibility, but I think the quiet that I go to when I meditate, I can bring that into the swirling river later on when I jump back into work."

And the river runs fiercely. Paul had 60 people reporting to him when he first started in early 2012, while at the time of this writing, he has 200. He's a manager of managers. Things are scaling up globally at a rapid pace. He feels pressure to produce results. "But I feel like I can do that in a way that's not inconsistent with my own values and with my meditation practice," he says.

Early Adoption

If we were to put it into product terms, we could say that Slakey represents the early portion of the adoption curve. You could think of mindfulness as a kind of fitness program for your consciousness, one that was formalized 2,500 years ago with Siddhartha Gautama, the Indian prince who would be referred to as the Buddha—"one who is awake." Though a religious structure grew around his teachings, it is not necessary to engage in any religiosity to meet mindfulness meditation. What could be less esoteric than simply sitting with attention placed on our bodies as we breathe in and out?

While it was developed to allow for the cessation of personal suffering, contemporary psychology uses the practice "as an approach for increasing awareness and responding skillfully to mental processes that contribute to emotional distress and maladaptive behavior," as psychologist and former University of Toronto assistant professor Scott R. Bishop noted.[3]

Practicing this has lasting consequences. A 2011 meta-analysis conducted by Harvard Medical School and Justus Liebig University of Germany consolidated decades of research into mindfulness, finding that the process had positive outcomes in attention regulation, body awareness, emotion regulation, and a change in the perception of the self. In short, mindfulness meditation allows you to better regulate your attention, be more aware of your body, more skillfully relate to your emotions, and—perhaps more startlingly—loosen your conception of self.[4] A Wake Forest University study found that mindfulness meditation can improve cognition after only four days of training.[5] A University of California, Santa Barbara study found that meditation increased working memory and reduced mental wandering. And breakthroughs in the understanding of neuroplasticity—that is, that the brain is able to change itself—show that by meditating, we can actually change the way our brains function.[6] And, equally as interesting, mindfulness practices change the very way our genes express themselves. Since we're exposing our minds to peace rather than stress, our bodies react accordingly.

What Is Mindfulness Meditation?

Bishop, the Canadian psychologist, supplies us a useful two-component definition of mindfulness: first to regulate attention to maintain focus on your immediate experience, and second to approach the phenomena of our experiences with curiosity, openness, and acceptance, regardless of how desirable you might find those phenomena to be.[7]

Essentially, by paying attention to our breath, we observe our internal and external stimuli—what's happening in us physiologically and emotionally, as well as what's going on in the environment, as *Atlantic* writer Liz Kulze noted.[8] Mindfulness allows us to have a more nuanced, articulate understanding of not only the events happening outside of our bodies but those happening within them.

As your authors have learned firsthand, and as the various mindfulness practitioners we've encountered in life have confirmed, one of the tools that all that sitting gives you is a little bit of a gap between you and your experiences, as Slakey observed. You become a more objective witness of your own experiences, seeing the way another person makes an action and then the way you are urged to respond, then acting in an unconditioned way. Instead of acting out our long-held tendencies, biases, and patterns, we can act in a way that serves the situation and the people involved.

These personal outcomes have major consequences for the way we work in organizations. If innovation arises from being able to see the same set of data in a new way, then practices that allow us to approach new situations with a fresh, unbiased, and slightly less conditioned state of mind are an asset. If we rely on our colleagues to share the things that cure our blind spots, then practices that deepen our relationships' apertures are an asset. If we need to be translating long-term goals into daily actions, then practices that allow us to introspect with more accuracy are an asset. If we simply need to better navigate the stressful stimuli of our days—the "swirling river" that Paul Slakey spoke of—then we need all the tools we can get.

This is one of the many riddles of our beloved *matryoshka* dolls. While we thought we were the centermost figure in this nested equation, there are layers even within ourselves. What a startling sensation! The contents of our identity show up in the interactions we have with our coworkers and team, in the emails we write, and in the products we create. If we tend to get frustrated when others do not understand a given subject as quickly as we do, there's probably a psychological reason for that. (Your authors may have experience with such hubristic, self-centered, self-defeating frustrations.)

In this way, getting familiar with our patterns of behavior lets us act more freely within the moment. If we know we tend to get frustrated in team discussions, then we can be on the lookout for that particular ego-istic bugbear as it arises, wave "hello" when it arrives, breathe deeply, and allow it to pass. However, that kind of internal dexterity is a skill that takes time to learn, in the same way hitting a baseball, an externally dexterous act, takes long hours of training. Meditation, then, is the batting cage for getting familiar with the fastballs and curveballs of our conscious and unconscious habits, which is precisely why we call it practice.

What Practice Looks Like

The Sanskrit word for mindfulness meditation is *shamatha*, which trans-lates directly as "calm abiding." The practice is not a method of capture but of releasing. There's a Zen saying that meditation stretches open the grasping hand of thought. And, as that image suggests, we become much more pliable and open with sitting practice. To describe it, we'll para-phrase the instructions given by American nun Pema Chödrön in her life-affirming *Start Where You Are.*[9]

1. Sit upright with your legs crossed. If you need to sit in a chair, make sure both feet are flat on the ground and straighten your spine—not straining it but allowing the spinal column to rest like a stack of coins. Rest your hands on your thighs.

2. Simply be aware of your breath as you exhale. Be "right there" with your breath as it goes out, with open focus that Chödrön says is "extremely relaxed" and "extremely soft," with about twenty-five percent of your attention resting on your breath.

Meditation

3. As you keep an awareness of your exiting breath, be aware of everything else your senses are telling you—the light on the walls, the sounds on the street, the taste in your mouth.

4. Thoughts will assuredly arise; you will certainly wander off. This is good! When you realize you are talking to yourself in your mind, you can show some compassion to yourself by simply saying to yourself, "thinking." Whether your thoughts are terrifying or pleasing, name them "thinking" with all your honesty and gentleness.

If you are starting meditation for the first time, appreciate that this is just a safari in your mind. You're not trying to "win" or "accomplish." You're just getting to know the neighborhood. And more than anything, give yourself the time to form the habit, for that is another component of devotion. Give meditation a trial run. Do the above practice for ten minutes every day for three weeks. See what happens. Get familiar. This familiarity requires a whole lot of devotion.

THE MOST IMPORTANT INGREDIENT FOR TRANSFORMING YOURSELF: DEVOTION

If we are going to find and release our blind spots, we need to be devoted.

Devotion is common to expert practitioners of any field, whether it's Larry Bird taking free throws late into the night or Howard Schultz roaming the streets of Milan and taking in the coffee culture. It's a hard-working creativity and a sense of craftsmanship. Taken from the Sanskrit word *bhakti*, Bengali gives us a beautiful word devotion: *shadhona*, or "life's pursuit with discipline."

I was born not too far from where Buddha was born. Sages and monks are still there debating about longing, suffering, and duties. With my affinity for Eastern philosophy, I find it is only when our devotion turns into discipline—and discipline into devotion—that we can begin to lead ourselves.

Devotion is composed of three parts: right effort, right mindfulness, and right concentration. These three qualities are mental development components within the traditional Buddhist teachings of the eight-fold path, which noted Brooklyn-born monk Bhikkhu Bodhi described in his lucid and concise *The Noble Eightfold Path*.[10]

Right Effort

Without effort, nothing can be achieved. As Bodhi writes, each person has to work out their own deliverance. No book, no teacher, no mentor, no organization, and no belief system can bring your work into the world for you. Putting your path into practice demands energy—and this is why effort is so crucial.

Right Mindfulness

We must know our minds directly. Mindfulness meditation allows us to train in observing our mental actions, though you do not need to be sitting on a cushion to be mindful. By closely attending to our experiences—both the parts we like and the parts we don't—we're able to develop an understanding that arises from ourselves. The Tibetan word for meditation is *gom*, or "familiarization." If we are going to live and lead with authenticity, we must become intimately familiar with our own minds in all of their many colors. As we discussed, this is a day-by-day practice.

Right Concentration

Concentration is unifying the mind. Even if you don't meditate, having a unified mind can be found in the engrossment of reading a good book— as we hope you are experiencing as you read this—and in the thrill of a long, hard run or the awe of taking in a brilliant summer sunset. When we have right concentration, our mental energy becomes focused like sunlight through a magnifying glass, strong enough to ignite fire.

Though our minds and days might wander off, we return to our task and our mission. Right concentration is coupled with effort and mindfulness. These three are all a single daily practice of understanding what your goals are as a leader. While we cannot control everything by an act of will, we can certainly be devoted to life's pursuit. And as a result, our personal devotion turns us into better leaders.

Refining our thinking, making the journey, ignoring the skeptics, and dusting ourselves off every time we fall requires disciplining our inner energy and drive. Thankfully, Western and Eastern contemplative traditions have handed down a variety of philosophies and practices for channeling and sustaining the energy with which we encounter the world.

Encountering Meditation

On a wintry New England day, I walked into a yoga studio in Stamford, Connecticut. I was part of a special meditation session led by Bhante Wimala, a Sri Lankan Buddhist monk. The studio smelled of incense and was well lit and intimate (it could hold no more than two dozen people). Bhante was sitting with his legs crossed into the lotus position and perched slightly above us on an elevated seating area. Walking in, it felt like I was in the presence of Siddhartha Gautama—the Buddha—himself. All walks of life—fathers, mothers, yogis, businessmen—were in attendance.

The Dalai Lama has praised Bhante, who has been traveling around the world and teaching, for his peace efforts. Bhante authored *Lessons of the Lotus*, a collection of his reflections on leading a wakeful and heartfelt life.[11] Over the course of two hours, Bhante walked us through the principle of living mindfully. He then led us through a thirty-minute session of mindfulness meditation, which focused on the sensations of breathing inward and outward, helping us abide openly in the moment.

After the sitting session, Bhante answered questions about life, death, purpose, authenticity, one's journey, and one's path. I was struck by how much these deep introspections corresponded to the questions we have about career and business, this endless asking of "What is the point?" "Who am I?" and "What am I here to do?" Upon reflecting, I can see that this internal work of knowing one's motivations and habits—you don't have to call it spirituality or even philosophy—inform and are informed by the work we share with the world. And when we consider that we live in a constantly transforming, ever-more-transparent world, it becomes increasingly obvious we need to do our business with authenticity, springing from a deep understanding of who we are, and mindfulness, a deep understanding of what is happening. We need to know the biases and habits we bring to each day; otherwise, we'll never even be aware of the blind spots that prevent us from connecting and innovating with the *oomph* of meaning.

IF YOU'RE GOING TO BE AUTHENTIC, YOU HAVE TO START FROM THE BOTTOM UP

Let's think back to the story of the Mayo Clinic from the last chapter. Here we have one of the great health care providers in the world, an organization at the forefront of its field. Instead of remaining in the routines that brought it to that privileged position, the organization journeyed into the frontier of its identity.

In bringing in IDEO to evaluate the patient experience, Mayo was able to reconsider its practice from the bottom up. This demonstrates that re-evaluation need not be a reaction to actual or imagined failure, but rather a kind of organizational hygiene, a spring cleaning of assumptions. And, consciously or not, Mayo's introspection is also a recognition of the fluidity of the world that businesses and customers participate in. Whether or not we hear them, Schumpeter's explosions are happening somewhere along our extended networks.

When we consider our business interactions, we can see there are four interconnected spheres: the leader, the organization, the ecosystem, and the customers. All of these spheres are connected. Eruptions happen in each and reverberate across all. This is why having intimacy with ourselves is so key. Understanding your interior life leads to understanding your exterior trajectory and allows you to take a more active role in its composition. In this way, understanding yourself is leading yourself.

To begin, let me tell you my story.

IN THE CORRIDORS OF CARBONDALE

It was August 1986. I was only seventeen and had recently arrived in America from Bangladesh. I was studying electrical engineering at Southern Illinois University in Carbondale. To survive, I quickly introduced myself to the art and science of "janitorial engineering" on the graveyard shift. Shortly after building my first commercial software product at age nineteen, I dropped out of college and joined Pitney Bowes. I later worked for multinationals such as General Electric, founded technology companies including KnowledgeBase and EC Cubed, and was part of a GE spin-off. To date, I have cumulatively raised tens of millions of dollars from angels, strategic partners, and institutional investors.

Like some founders, I, too, got ousted from serving as CEO of my own company EC Cubed, and I survived recession after recession. Regardless of the situation, I have never abandoned my entrepreneurial spirit.

Over the years, I have realized that life is a process of ongoing transformation, spurred on by the interlinked qualities of curiosity, purpose, and courage. Whether or not we ask it to, the journey of life tends to make us strong, teaches us to contribute to the best of our abilities, and allows us to pursue a personal legend according to our own terms.

This is not a new impulse. Joseph Campbell helps us to see why.[12] A student of Carl Jung, who himself was a student of Sigmund Freud, Campbell founded a new and crucial field when he was flourishing in 1960s and '70s America: comparative mythology. Mythology and fairy tales, as he reads them, are not just bedtime stories—though they are surely that. Instead, they are notes that previous cultures have left us about how to live life, how to take care of one another, and where to find meaning. To ignore myth is to commit a great act of hubris. Though technology has accelerated and, in some cases, modified human interactions, the questions of love, fulfillment, and ontological mystery that the debaters of Athens, the roundtables of the Algonquin, or the tribes of the Amazon—the great questions of *Who Am I?* and *What Am I to Do?*—renew themselves in every generation and every individual.

WHAT DOES IT MEAN TO KNOW YOURSELF?

As Westerners, we have a rich history of individuality. "Know thyself" was inscribed across the Oracle of Delphi's door. Powerful arguments have been made about the source of this impulse. In *The Geography of Thought*, comparative psychologist Richard Nisbett observes that Ancient Greece, the prototypical individualist culture, developed in a jagged, mountainous land where people were separated by their environment, encouraging a diversity-prizing culture to develop. Ancient China, the prototypical collectivist culture, developed in broad plains isolated by the mountains and the sea, leading to a harmony-prizing culture. The book is a must-read for anyone on either side of modern East-West interactions.[13]

If the Oracle's dictum is a distillation of the oldest Western culture, modern Westerners would do well to consider it. This self-knowledge has become a kind of New Age cure-all to all sorts of dilemmas, and for good reason. Our decisions spring from our understanding of the way our experience interacts with the world. We call this experience my self, my identity, myself. And yet that's where these discussions end, for language only goes so far. While knowing thyself is, in part, a linguistic endeavor—writing and reading certainly help—it is nonlinguistic, even non-conceptual. It demands observing and becoming intimate with your actions, your habits, and your motivations. This quest for self-understanding is precisely at the center of our intercultural conversations about mindfulness, a conversation that's crucial to enter into if we are to transform our working lives. In this way, we can unite the complementary contrasts of West and East.

Of course, we won't be "solving" this "problem" in the following pages. Rather, let's go for the more resolvable task of opening a few illuminating discussions that will hopefully cure a handful of our blind spots. And naturally, we'll start with the core of the argument—authenticity.

"Authenticity" comes from the Greek root *authentikos*, meaning "original, genuine, principal." Genuine leaders go beyond (and certainly precede) the usual pantheon of business chieftains, historical figures, and mega technology innovators. They are all around us. To be authentic, you must be "awake," meaning you have the ability to understand who you are, what you want to be, and how you want to fit into the world.

From Aristotle to Siddhartha Gautama, Rumi to Steve Jobs, and Khalil Gibran to Paulo Coelho, thinkers and poets have said that the path to authentic journey is to intimately know who you are. Nietzsche wrote of becoming your most true self; positive psychologists speak of self-realization; a Zen koan asks what your face looked like before your parents were born. As David Whyte observes in *Crossing the Unknown Sea: Work as a Pilgrimage of Identity*, work is an extension and expression of self.[14] But what is it to know yourself?

The process of self-discovery—especially for the leader—unites the ancient ideals of the *vita activa* (active life) and *vita contemplativa* (contemplative life). To have balance, we must have a balance of doing and reflecting, a movement between investigation and withdrawal, even within a day. As research psychologist Barbara Fredrickson has uncovered, becoming more aware of ourselves allows us to better connect with those around us. And as Michael Schrage writes in *Who Do You Want Your Customers to Become?*, better understanding yourself allows you to better connect with your customer.[15] And by becoming more aware of ourselves, we can encourage whatever's waiting inside of us to come into the world, our individual genius.

In his ass-kicking *The War of Art*, Steven Pressfield calls upon the Classical notion of the genius. For Pressfield, rather than the province of Einstein, Jobs, or Picasso, genius is something endowed in each of us:

> "Genius is a Latin word; the Romans used it to denote an inner spirit, holy and inviolable, which watches over us, guiding us to our calling. A writer writes with his *genius*; an artist paints with hers; everyone who creates operates from this sacramental center. It is our soul's seat, the vessel that holds our being-in-potential, our star's beacon and Polaris."[16]

Isn't this idea of genius beautiful? Of a kind of creative soul? It's fascinating to think about how Western culture gives us this ideal of the signature individual creative act. In making something, be it business, book, or painting, we bring something into the world that could only come from us. Joseph Campbell, the mythologist mentioned before, described this as the great Western truth: that each individual has something precisely their own to offer. The thing is, though, figuring what exactly that entails is often like biting your own teeth.

This is where mindfulness is so helpful. Not that it helps us bite our teeth—there might be other meditations for that—but that it helps us to better see the action happening within our minds. When you become a better observer of your own doings, you naturally develop a more realistic sense of yourself. Maybe you aren't actually so nice to your colleagues all the time, and maybe you shouldn't have a guilt spiral because you do. Maybe you're more worried about that deadline than you let on, and maybe you can admit to yourself that you need to talk to a trusted friend about it. Mindfulness helps us to see the ways our actions aren't in correlation with the ideals we have about ourselves. In this way, it helps us become more aware of our own interior states, which leads to being more empathic for others and more authentic. And from that authenticity, we become more trustworthy, more truly confident, and more well-rounded.

TAKING RESPONSIBILITY: DEVELOPMENT AS INTEGRATION

To be a leader is to have trust in one's journey. Nietzsche has a Latin line for it: *amor fati*: the love of fate.[17] As entrepreneurs, we need to love ours.

As we shall see, this isn't necessarily a self-centered venture. As the research psychologist Mihaly Csikszentmihalyi encapsulates near the end of his must-read *Flow*, we construct what we want to achieve in life—our destinies—in a series of shifts of perspectives.[18] We begin by needing to preserve ourselves, to survive. When the physical self is secure, we can expand our perspective to an in-group, like a family, community, or in rare cases, a company, and take the values of the group to be the values of the individual. The third phase is "reflexive individualism," in which the person turns inward, develops an autonomous consciousness, and desires growth and actualization. The fourth and final stage is a "final turning away" from the self and an integration into the collective; the interests of the individual are merged with the whole. This is, the psychologist says, a dialectic movement of differentiation and integration between withdrawal into the self and union with the collective.

This developmental pendulum is of great interest to leaders. Back in Carbondale, Illinois, I entered into graveyard-shift entrepreneurship by default. It was a matter of survival. As well, we can frequently find ourselves among those that stay comfortably in the second stage. You have the feeling that those who desire the security of the "company man" are seeking to reside in the comfort of organizational identity. That third stage, I think, is especially prevalent in entrepreneurs. We chide "yes men" and exhort one another upon our individualistic quests (notice how "differentiation" is one of the emergent marketing buzzwords).

What we hope to do in this book is encourage you and your company to enter into that fourth stage of development, to reunite with the world. This is often seen by the greatly successful later in life. Having fulfilled their individualistic ambitions, they throw their expertise into world-enriching endeavors, the most obvious of which are the efforts of Bill and Melinda Gates to eradicate diseases and reform education. But this does not have to be so gigantic. Teaching your expertise, becoming a mentor to others—this is the stuff of integrated, mature development. Having turned inward, the more we grow, the more we turn outward.

The most effective businesses, as Clay Christensen argued in *The Innovator's Dilemma*, are those that sense customers' unvoiced or unmet needs and provide for them. As Ron Adner describes in *The Wide Lens*,[19] the understanding of ecosystem is a turn away from egocentric, isolated invention. Rather, it recognizes that the interdependent integration of any product—for the success of any product, regardless of the company that sells it—depends on an array of interlocked factors. In this way, innovation becomes an empathic act. The leader, through a variety of mechanisms, understands herself, the company, the ecosystem, and the customer well enough to provide products that create value for all parties involved.

What's important, then, is to realize that these qualities of mindfulness, authenticity, and empathy can be developed—with practice.

TAKEAWAYS

Understanding is the foundation. The better we understand the nature of the world, the better we can move in the world. The better we understand the nature of ourselves, the better we can move within ourselves. This is why generations of thinkers and doers have told us in a multitude of ways to know ourselves—an intrapersonal intimacy that is the fruit of a long process.

Understanding leads to authenticity. When you know yourself, you can act with a confidence that is your own. This implies a rawness and vulnerability to the people around you—which is a very good thing, as that vulnerability is the foundation of the relationships that define us.

Devotion is mindfulness, mindfulness is devotion. You do not become strong by lifting one gigantic weight. You do not understand yourself by reading one book or attending a workshop. It is a daily practice of devotion. Devotion is our sustainable resource. With it, we can, day by day, improve ourselves, our teams, and our world.

CHAPTER 3

WHAT WE TALK ABOUT WHEN WE TALK ABOUT WORKING TOGETHER

"Each friend represents a world in us."
—Anaïs Nin[1]

The Three Blind Men

STOP US IF YOU'VE heard this one before. You and three friends are in the back room of a tavern. Since this is the 13th century, there isn't any electricity. The space is lit by half a dozen candles. In the next room, there is an elephant, though none of you have seen such a beast before. You've all heard conflicting tales about this beast; none of you know exactly what one looks like. You're all determined to find out what this lauded animal is, but the room's only big enough to fit one of you at a time. So, one by one, you go inside. The thing is, you have to go in blindfolded.

With eyes covered, the first enters.

After a while, he returns.

The room was too dark to see the elephant, he says, and the blindfold didn't help. He felt for the animal with his hands, which he now stretches wide. "An elephant is long, thick as a rope, and flexible," he reports, "like a water pipe."

"That's not like the elephants I've heard of," you think to yourself.

The second takes the blindfold and goes in.

He reemerges.

"An elephant is broad, thin, and flops when I hold it," he says. "It must be a fan."

The first friend defends his claim that an elephant is like a water pipe, not a fan. The second insists that an elephant is floppy by nature. The conversation between the two does not move toward a resolution.

Wanting to put an end to the matter, the third friend enters the room, comes back, then shouts, "No! An elephant is broad, thick, and heavy, just like a great temple pillar!"

Neither of the first two explorers is impressed.

So, you decide to take the elephant into your own hands.

You walk into the dark room, wondering why you had to put a blind-fold on—it seems redundant.

No matter. You hear the rustle of a large animal, though you can't determine exactly what is making the noise. You feel a great heat, but you can't tell exactly where the heat is coming from. And you smell something foul. You reach your hand out for this elephant, landing upon something narrow. It flops about like a reed in the wind. An elephant, it seems, is something like a stiff, strange, smelly snake.

You tell as much to your friends, who disagree with you into the night.

WHAT WERE YOU FEELING?

The above story is an old one. Hindus, Jains, Buddhists, and Sufis all tell versions of it. In our telling, the first friend felt the elephant's trunk, the second, its ear, the third, its knee, and you, my dear investigator, felt the great beast's tail (and smelled its generous backside). As with the best tales, this one has many interpretations.

We'll focus on one reading, as told by the Sufi poet-saint Rumi.[2] You and your friends each represent how a person accesses reality (what we usually refer to when we say "the truth"). This interpretation itself has many applications, but let's focus in on what it means for enterprise. First, each of us is pretty staggeringly ignorant, no matter the education and experiences we've had. The quickest way to work around our own unique sets of ignorance is to have the trust and counsel of people who know things we don't. Some people access the truth as an elephant's ear, others as its tail. As people trying to do meaningful, daresay truthful work, we need as many hands on the elephant as possible.

You can also think of each friend as a different discipline; each touches a different aspect of the elephant in the room. Is one more valid than the other? Probably not. How would you get a better idea of the nature of an elephant? By combining ideas, perspectives, and skills—by cooperating. To understand the elephant in the room, we have to partner together.

ON PARTNERSHIP

Each person and discipline accesses the world through their own perspectives, carrying narratives and baggage they do and do not see. Our upbringing, our education, and our disciplines shape us as we shape them. This snowflake-like individuality showcases how each person has a unique potential but also a unique ignorance. We cannot escape our own perspectives, which is why, if we want to do good work—and particularly if we want to innovate—we need to have other trusted hands on the elephant.

We need to have people with us who can touch this same elephant and communicate their experiences. No matter what your analytical capability might be, the power of your Google intuition, or the extent of your erudition, you cannot get around your gender, ethnicity, socioeconomic class, and other inborn factors. These all limit your understanding. You can only have one, or if you're lucky, two hands on the elephant. And to do great work, we need many more. We need a team.

This chapter is an investigation into how we can combine our efforts to understand this elephant called working life. We'll discuss what we refer to as "partnerships"—the kind of relationships that allow people to do their best work. As well, we'll investigate how to act in a way that benefits all parties involved. To accomplish these ambitions, we'll discuss the evolutionary underpinnings at work when we're working, articulate the aspects of work culture that hinder partnerships, and describe the nuts and bolts of partnership formation. But before we get to that, let's discuss partnership and why it's so crucial to continual innovation.

The Partnership Principle

A partnership is a bond. A mutual investment. A relationship. A voluntary, collaborative agreement. Partnerships are crucial because, as leadership scholar Don Peppers writes, "trust is a lubricant for transactions."[3] We no longer work in an era where we're trying to make everything as efficient as possible. Rather, we're trying to be more agile, more innovative, and to move quicker with our iterations. This means we need to work together.

In the same way that a blueprint predicts and informs the creation of a building but cannot know its daily maintenance, or in the same way vows predict and inform a marriage but cannot know its daily incarnations, vision statements and org charts can predict and inform the daily events of working life. But, since each day has never happened before, there is no constellation of best practices that we can defer our responsibility to in the decisions that we make and in the interactions that we have in our working lives. The best grounding is an intent.

Since we must continually create value that moves with our customers' shifting behaviors, and since we must be able to be with the people we work with every day—more than our spouses, friends, and families in most cases—we must hold ourselves accountable to our intention every day. The intention, the aspiration for our work environments, if they are going to create maximum value, is to have one of mutual flourishing.

The ancient Greeks knew this. They did not mark their lives by years of birth or death, but rather by the years of flourishing (such as between the ages of thirty-five and forty-five). Today, we refer to this as one's "prime" or perhaps "maximal earning years." It's the time when you are, in other words, at the height of your powers. In his *Ethics*, Aristotle takes a hard look at human flourishing. He refers to *eudaimonia* (taking from the prefix *eu-*, good, as in euphoria, and *daimon*, or spirit) as "virtuous activity in accordance with reason,"[4] another way of expressing the link between short term and long term, between mindfulness and authenticity.

Flourishing is starting to show up in business literature: of being fully there, fully invested in work, and working in productive teams. We tend to call this "employee engagement." It has results. A 2012 Towers Watson study showed that the firms involved with "high sustainable engagement"—which they qualify as driven by culture and work relationships—have an average annual operating margin triple that of their less-engaged peers.[5] In addition, a 2012 report from McKinsey showed that organizations with the highest levels of motivation were sixty percent more likely to place themselves in the top twenty-five percent of overall business health. Again, the qualitative shapes the quantitative.[6]

It looks like we are at an organizational inflection point, with the early adopters beginning to structure their workplaces around wellness. We'll expand on how to holistically structure an organization later on. For now, let us focus on how our human interactions inform our flourishing. To do this, we'll need to take a deep look at what's happening psychologically within our business lives. The patterns of interaction predate capitalism.

Reptiles and Mammals

We use the phrase "office culture" to describe many things. Regardless of the slogans plastered across the walls, the actual ambiance of a place arises from interactions that happen there. And if we're not aware of our actions, we unknowingly create patterns of behavior that might be unhealthy without being able to reflect on them. So, it's in our favor to describe our habitats. To get a handle on how relationships do or don't form, let's take a look at the behavioral history present here.

Consider reptiles and mammals. Which kingdom has shown itself to be more innovative? While we may be biased with our hair and our milk and all, it seems a safe claim to say that mammals are more innovative than their scaly counterparts. There's a reason that crocodiles, even after their millions of years on the planet, don't use tools as we apes do.

Yet, if you've been to an office full of internet-addled workers, you might find that the people there are less like their ape cousins that pick the bugs out of each other's hair and more like alligators that eat their young on an impulse. Who would develop more interesting products— the mammals or the reptiles?

You've probably heard the phrase "lizard brain" bandied about before.[7]

Stephen Porges's research helps us refine our understanding a little more. According to Porges—who's published more than 200 academic journal articles and has been formative in the development of evolutionary neurophysiology—consciousness is a system of interlocking levels, each reflecting different stages of our evolution. That's why, at a primal level so basic it's outside the range of perception, a part of you is looking out for danger while more contemporary parts of ourselves help us relate to others, plan for the future, and (critical for innovation) invent tools. The reptilian mind protects; the mammalian mind connects.

Two activities fundamental to bringing about innovation—working together and entertaining new ideas—can only happen when that reptilian part of ourselves deems the situation safe. You're not going to be able to be reflective of your past, predictive of the future, or mindful of the present if a prehistoric part of you thinks there's a predator around. Even if you're not conscious of it, you'll be limited to acting like a reptile. Why? Because that reptilian mind is mostly concerned with keeping us alive.

Whether you're aware of it or not, a level of your consciousness is vigilantly looking out for anything that might be going awry. Without that sentry sense detecting a threshold of security, Porges says you won't be able to relate closely to people or work creatively. Notice yourself if you have vibrations or loud ventilation shafts in your office and contrast your state of mind and productivity with when you have pleasant sounds around you. That ventilation shaft rumble upsets the reptilian mind, which makes us less apt to be prosocial or creative and more likely to close off and protect.

Do You Work with Mammals or Reptiles?

Think about the reptile way of life. You're profoundly alone. No one is around to look out for you. A reptilian corporate style, Porges tells us, is one embedded in defense and fear. You experience life as scarcity—there are never enough resources to make you secure—and the furthest you'll project into the future is whether or not you'll survive the day. A reptilian office has a tough time creating because fear hamstrings innovation. New ideas and other forms of change are signs of volatility, which are signs of danger to the reptile.

But a mammalian habitat would have a different ambiance. Management would acknowledge everyone is in it together, Porges says. As such, we would make the workplace a safe place for the collective. And since their working lives feel consistent, stable, and secure, employees can bring in the volatility of bold thinking, which would cause a panic in a scalier system. This is why mammals are better innovators. If you want people to just act, act, act, then scaring them can be useful for short-term productivity. But if you want them to make better products, then you have to quash any sense of zero-sum culture.

Since innovation, as the pyrotechnic language we use to describe it suggests, is an unpredictable and highly volatile pursuit, then at a base level, our minds read it as "danger." It makes sense that humans who are already experiencing elements of danger, be it in the form of a lack of job security, emotionally abusive management, or imprisonment to metrics, wouldn't be able to handle bringing in the additional volatility implied in experimentation, exploration, or any of the other vulnerability-making drivers of innovation. The safer we make the workplace, the more dangerous ideas we can develop there. If we want our people to make stuff explode, we need to give them a safe place to do so.

A lot of that safety has to do with time.

What Time Is It?

About a hundred years ago, a French philosopher, Henri Bergson, was the toast of the English-speaking world. His thought reached, affected, and reflected all the corners of Parisian culture at that time, from the stream-of-consciousness novel to impressionist paintings. He was a pithy fellow, once quipping that the duty of the philosopher was to make the implicit into the explicit—an emphasis on articulation that we aspire to ourselves. And, as the wise often do, Bergson reevaluated the most fundamental of things, such as time itself.

Beyond being a great aphorist, he had a profound and unique understanding of the nature of time. He criticized "clock time" as being tyrannical and imprecise. It might be useful, perhaps, for scientific research, but not for living. Rather, a more precise notion of time is best left untranslated, as he thought of time as *durée*, which could be clumsily translated as "duration." Instead of time being this thing on the wall or on the watch, time is your ongoing, fluid experience; your consciousness.[8]

If we use Bergson's lens to understand these things, we can then make the conclusion that management of tasks is actually management of time, which is actually management of consciousness. That is to say, when you're trying to get people on the same schedule (or not), you're talking about managing their consciousness, their experience of life. Which is really quite the thing, isn't it?

But revolting against the tyranny of clock time is not just for impressionist-era philosophers. It's also for modern-day ultra-doers like Bob Pozen, who once simultaneously served as president of Fidelity Investments, taught a full course load at Harvard Business School, and penned articles for *Harvard Business Review*. In one such piece, he contended that a bias toward valuing workers by the hours they put in (which studies have shown managers do) was exceptionally misguided.[9] To Pozen, professionals aren't valuable to a company for the hours they put in—which engenders a culture privileging "face time"—but for the "value they create through their knowledge." And since the measure of quality lies in hours rather than results, Pozen says managers distract their workers from the most critical question—"Am I currently using my time in the best possible way?" The result is that they use their time inefficiently.

Let's expand his argument to a philosophical level. By privileging hours over results, we distract ourselves from asking if we're using our minds in the best possible way, resulting in a culture that is only accidentally mindful—if at all. Adapting our working lives around the hours we put in is a way of avoiding the responsibility of using our consciousness and our energy in the best possible way. Orienting around the end product (and present process) helps us to be more rigorous with how we align our experiences with our outcomes. What's wondrous about working in an organization is that there is a whole bunch of consciousness involved, the many people who are alive and thinking and feeling and having fears and insights and pressures and triumphs.

One of the foundational steps to working in a prosocial, commitment-oriented, mammalian way is to recognize that the people we're working with have also had long experiences with life—experiences you haven't had—that will yield insights you can't have. To paraphrase the author and diarist Anaïs Nin, each person represents a world—and if we are here to do work that changes the world, we need the people we work with to share theirs. Yet this requires a rhythm of working in a group and working alone.[10]

As Pozen suggests, a lot of guarding your time comes down to being able to say "no" and express priorities, which means you need to have a culture that's comfortable with open conversation and saying, "No, actually. I can't do that." If you are going to have an adaptable organization, the people need to be able to adapt. If the people are going to adapt, they need to be able to control their time. To do that, they need to be able to communicate. That is the path to shared endeavor, to partnership.[11]

How Einstein Managed Time

Relentless Innovation author Jeffrey Phillips favors a line from Einstein. The story is that Einstein was asked how he would tackle a particularly tough problem—saving the world, in some tellings—if he only had an hour to do so.[12] Einstein's approach? He'd spend fifty-five minutes defining the problem and five minutes solving it, which is, Phillips says, just about the opposite of what executives normally do. He paints a picture of harried execs deciding immediately on a solution, launching into its implementation, and then cooling down with email. It's all task, task, task—symptomatic of a work culture that's getting too busy to innovate, that's become infatuated with efficiency. We might be doing something with our time, but are we developing?

As Phillips argues, our busyness begets "a foreshortening of time." We are habitually busy, and so we focus on the next activity, next day, and next fire rather than being able to give time to issues that require deep concentration. Being mired in tasks becomes the normal thing to do. This is what happens when the quantitative has a stranglehold on the qualitative, when we don't understand the ways that the *matryoshka* dolls nest inside of one another. As Einstein's quip suggests, the framing of the question is an outsized portion of the solution-finding process. And as Clay Christensen once told us, when you ask the right question, the answer becomes mechanical. Clearly, we need to be privileging that process—which has a rhythm of introspection and collaboration—throughout our processes.

Who does a good job of creating space for thought? With its emphasis on having a "palette of place" for choosing an environment for the work that is necessary, the furniture manufacturer Steelcase provides its team the flexibility to recognize when they need to protect their time and dive uninterrupted into deep-thinking problems.[13] This can be as simple as being able to choose to work from home or in the office. If you need to dive deeply into your work, then stepping away from the office and into your home or a third space like a café works well. Your environment is a tool; just as you need the right tool for the job, we'd do well to find the right environment for the job.

Fabrica, a production company with Benetton, shows this as well. It outfitted its Italian villa—yes, that's where employees work—to have both thoroughly connected spaces and purposefully dead signal zones. He notes that just as "noise is meaningless without quiet, connectivity becomes meaningless when pervasive," which shows that it is possible to create a work culture that appreciates the presence of absence.[14] It also shows that part of partnership is allowing people to find the environments that enable them to do their best work and provide the alignment and resources that allow them to do so autonomously, which we'll discuss at length in the next section.

Time, Stimulation, and Success

Leslie Perlow has spent her career researching the micro-dynamics of work. Once a management consultant, she has since moved into academia and is now a professor of leadership at Harvard Business School. She recently authored *Sleeping with Your Smartphone*, a book that distills the insights she gleaned while researching the perpetually swamped Boston Consulting Group. Her research shows how even the most extreme of work cultures can shift their behavior.[15]

Like where people declare themselves to be addicts, where the label "workaholic" is worn like a badge of courage, and to be otherwise is to appear lazy, unproductive, and not-team-oriented. From reading Perlow's work and speaking with her, we came to agree with her realization that the high achievers she studied were not addicted to the work they do, but rather to the feelings of success and validation they gained from it, like the momentary satisfaction of a beeping phone. We are creatures of—and sometimes victims to—our feedback loops.

Recognizing this, Perlow helped BCG to revise its feedback loops. For one of the BCG teams she was studying, an agreement was made that each person would have one night off a week where they wouldn't do any work. They would not even glance at their phones, even if a big deliverable appeared for the next day. That was the agreement. To reinforce this, feedback shifted accordingly. Instead of employees coming in and being told "good job" if they worked late into their night off, they'd get a slap on the wrist for going against the team's agreement. Finally, team members could turn off without the itch to check in.

But this kind of change doesn't happen by sloganeering. Imagine the resentment that would build if a team leader walked into a weekly meeting and shouted, "Everyone's getting a night off!" Instead, to make this kind of shift happen, we need to take a more subtle tack.

That initial questioning becomes a lever for opening a larger conversation. Instead of putting everyone in a room and saying, "Now we're going to talk about taking more time off," you begin a discussion about what's the biggest bugbear for a team. It could be unpredictability (like for BCG), or it could be having days of endless meetings. Then, bring the discussion to a point of mutual agreement for how to deal with that problem. It could be a night fully unplugged, or it could be a meeting-free day of working from home. Make sure that your solution is measurable. You'll know if you didn't unplug or if you did have a meeting. By opening up the discussions, finding a solution, and recording its implementation, Perlow says we don't just get a grip on tracking the work, but we can also reflect on how the work gets done. This is a way for everybody in the group to find and exchange feedback, which, in turn, allows us to grow our teams' understanding of the way it works.

Perlow, Pozen, Bergson, and Porges all help us recognize similar points. To work closely together is to respect one another's time and to respect one another's consciousness. Of course, consciousness feels overwhelming a lot of the time. This is another reason the bonds of partnership are so key. The way we get through the trials of professional life is not only by training ourselves to take better care of ourselves individually—which mindfulness is so powerful in helping us to do—but also in relying upon one another. As we'll explore further in the following chapters, one of the primary predictors of success for a team is the quality and quantity of human connections people have. We call these deep connections partnerships. A partnership is founded on respect for the other person's consciousness.

KEYSTONES TO BUILDING PARTNERSHIPS

Success begins with people. To better take care of yours, review the following principles.

Be Honest

It's the best and only policy when communicating with a potential customer, client, colleague, employee, supplier, distributor, contractor, or even an industry rival. And it's the same policy whether you're speaking face-to-face, across the board table, or via text or tweet. You must be honest with yourself, your audience, and your mission. It's easy to insulate ourselves from the truth (thus, the authenticity exercises of the previous chapter). Effective leaders must be honest in order to create trust and respect within their team and with anyone they encounter. Be good to people. Business is a lifelong endeavor, and you never know who you will have to rely on or turn to in the future.

Be Direct

Direct communication leads to direction, meaning the path you set as a leader. Nobody wants to follow a muddled message, even if they could. Every word must be deliberate and directed. Don't be tempted to reach out without direction, which can deter or even destroy your overall agenda. If you can't say something clearly and directly, wait until you can articulate it to yourself. Talk may be cheap, but it can be worthless if uttered without direction. It can even cost you a client, a deal, or your whole business. A direct message is priceless; as E. B. White writes in the timeless *The Elements of Style*, "every word must tell."[16]

Think Ahead

No matter how successful you are, you won't continue on that golden path if you stop anticipating what's next, which is a job too big to do on your own. You need to surround yourself with forward-thinkers. A single team member that's complacent can drag everyone involved into a downward spiral. Make sure your people are ready for changes, even the most unprecedented challenges. Think back on Schumpeter's explosions and the interconnectedness of our many enterprises. Changes are constant. Since you can trust that what you're doing today will be wrong tomorrow, you need to forge trusting, resilient teams that minimize their decision costs.

Inspire and Influence

The most successful leaders are able to inspire and influence everyone from their executive team to their employees, customers, clients, partners, investors, and beyond. Inspiration cannot happen without clear communication. You have to show people you're a person, too. Success can quickly inflate egos to the point of isolation of leadership and alienation of those who are most critical to your ongoing ability to survive and thrive. The best and brightest will be toppled if they can't inspire others. It takes a dynamic person with a positive, honest, forward-looking attitude to inspire and influence the people involved in building and growing enterprises and communities.

Create a Community

As with any community, a healthy business ecosystem must be nurtured to achieve continual success. A sustainable ecosystem is the structure you form around your business. Those interconnections allow us to bring in individuals and groups, exposing you and your team to ideas and perspectives they wouldn't have encountered otherwise, creating synergistic cross-pollinations. The interoperability enables collaboration, whether with your neighbor, your C-suite counterparts, or potential customers across the world. This is what I focus on every day within my own company and with everyone I encounter. You must always be open to inviting new people into your extended enterprise, for its potential never ends.

Think Long Term

Focusing on quarterly earnings is a diversion from the long-term picture, which includes the overall health of a company, cash flow, and the ability to stay in business. While it may feel counterintuitive to thrive within a volatile world, leaders must be aware of the present moment and set their sights on long-term goals. Since value creation is qualitative as well as quantitative, no metric can completely capture success. Volatile times can't be avoided, but you can be ready for disruption in the marketplace or your own life with a long-term plan and network that supports your vision and enables you to bring to market the right product and make the right decisions for your lifelong satisfaction.

TAKEAWAYS

An organization is its people. And people are mammals. There's no getting around the fact that humans are humans—and not only that, but we have an evolutionary legacy that walks around with us. Working in the 21st century doesn't change that. We need to be aware of the way our psychological legacy manifests itself in us, to catch ourselves when we're acting like alligators, and take pride in being mammals, as silly as it sounds.

Management is time management. And time management is consciousness management. If we want our teams to be creative, we need to provide for them the time and space to do the work they need to get done. We also need to have a culture where it's normal to give voice to concerns.

An organization is a partnership. If you want to get the best out of your team, they need to feel invested in their mission and invested in you. You can only do this by showing that you are investing in them, not as "resources" or "talent," but as people with complete lives. You cannot tell a flower to grow, but you can provide the environment for it to bloom. It is the same case with us.

CHAPTER 4

LONG-TERM PLANS, DYNAMIC PRESENT

"Do you have the patience to wait till your mud settles and the water is clear?"
—*Lao Tzu*[1]

AN EXPERIMENT: A FOUR-YEAR-OLD girl sits at a desk in a California school. An array of treats—marshmallows, cookies, other confections—is spread out before her. A researcher asks her to select a sweet; she chooses a marshmallow. Then, a proposition. She can either eat the lone marshmallow now or have two if she waits for him to come back after a few minutes. What does she do?

According to *The New Yorker*, she—a young Carolyn Weisz—waited. Her brother Craig, also part of the experiment, didn't. Decades later, the siblings found themselves in divergent places. Carolyn became a professor, while Craig did "all kinds of things" in the entertainment industry but didn't make it far. He could have made better career choices, he says.[2]

Carolyn and Craig were part of what's now affectionately (and confection-ately) known as the Marshmallow Experiment, which happened at the Bing Nursery School at Stanford University. The subjects were revisited in follow-up studies, and the thirty percent who were able to delay gratification at that nursery school table were linked with having higher SAT scores in adolescence and lower Body Mass Indexes in adulthood. While we are indeed inferring, the research suggests that delaying gratification—or, in other words, thinking long term—predicts higher functioning down the line.

This carries over to the development of our working life as well. In the nursery school experiment of the C-suite, short-term profits are the marshmallows that test our wills. And with the pressures from investors and shareholders, there's plenty of outside motivation to gobble up that glucose. But if we want to be intelligent and fit in the long run, we have to resist that temptation. Rather than trying to capture short-term profit, we create long-term value.

CONCERNING VALUE AND INNOVATION

A word is an image of an image. When you read the word *cat*, the feline and feelings that occur to you are different than the person next to you. The collection of experiences you associate with *cat* inform what you hold a cat to be. This is the origin of why people say they do or don't like such a creature or other type. While there's a lexical functionality to agreeing that cats are mostly furry, four-legged, and clawed creatures, what constitutes "catness" exists only in the person thinking on what a cat may be.

As well, the connotations of *"cat"* vary in their cultural context. If you're in a place where jaguars are more likely to be spotted predators than luxury sedans, the emotional content of *"cat"* will be much different than a city dweller who knows automobiles better than living creatures. What's fascinating is how a vocabulary evolves with a culture. Being that we are now in the innovation economy rather than the efficiency economy, we need to recast a few of our definitions. We're playing fast and loose with the philosophy of language here, but trust us, there's a point.

We need to consider this idea of creating value. The phrase comes up again and again in business literature and conferences, but we disagree on what value is. It's no wonder. Humans have been encountering cats for millennia, but we still have an individual, culturally informed account of what constitutes "catness." And "value" in the business sense has only been bandied about for so long (capitalism, as we know it, is still pretty young).

The Economist, the staid British publication of wryness and polite charm, recently provided a history of this most crucial of buzzwords. And we do mean crucial. Where an organization creates value is at the crux of any enterprise's operations. "Value creation is a corporation's *raison d'être*," the article begins. "The ultimate measure by which it is judged." According to the article, value creation has a number of possible meanings. It could be the value the stock market assigns the company, the value shown on the balance sheet, or profits or cash expected on future performance, or, perhaps, none of these.[3]

There are holes in each definition. If you decide that the value of the company is measured by its stock price, that doesn't take into account the macroeconomic swirls of the market (recall the rapid stock inflation of the dot-com boom). And the bookkeeper's measure does not totally capture value either. Intangible assets like brand identification and patents do not show up on a balance sheet. As well, predictive valuation smells very much of hubris. Categorically, you cannot access an entity at any time but the present. If these measures don't work, how can we get a sense of value?

The Rhythm of Need and Value

Let's return to that Zen cup from earlier. This time, rather than the vessel representing your state of mind, it represents your customers' needs—a gap not yet filled, a job to be done. When we fill our customers' needs, we create value for them. One of Clay Christensen's favorite ideas about innovation is the notion of "jobs-to-be-done." He posits that the reason someone buys a product is because they are hiring it to perform some task for them. Take the humble milkshake, for instance. His team's research found that many people bought milkshakes for their commute since it was a long-lasting, delicious experience. Plus, unlike a doughnut, it wouldn't run the risk of getting all over them.[4]

In this way, creating value for a customer is a kind of listening. Just as in a romantic relationship, you can be a better partner by listening for what the other person wants or needs—and this, we know, isn't always vocalized. Continuously creating value is a kind of long-term listening. When we see a need beginning to be expressed, we can move in a way that allows that want to be filled, as the story of how UPS grew its Service Parts Logistics division. And as the prescient Jeff Bezos reminds us, that transaction cannot occur unless trust is already established. Listening drives trust, trust drives partnership, partnership drives value creation. And as we will see shortly, these are all elements of long-term thinking.

Additionally, the truly sustainable company not only considers the jobs its customers hire its products to do, but also considers the jobs that its employees hire it to do. It's important now to note that earning a salary is only one component of the reason people work. They need to advance their careers, create meaning in their lives, and gain validation from their peers, to name a few. And since the highest-functioning companies have the highest-functioning employees, leaders would do well to fill their employees' needs as well, though those needs, like those of the milkshake-drinking commuters, may not be obvious. That intra-organizational partnership will be the core of this book's next section. But before we can zoom in, we need to zoom out.

VISION: WHAT ARE WE HERE TO DO?

Legacy

"Eventually, a man turns thirty," the French philosopher Albert Camus wrote in *The Myth of Sisyphus*, "and he realizes that he belongs to time."[5] And time, of course, is a death sentence. Every human—and every human creation—perishes. Countless kingdoms never left a trace and are totally gone. A corporation (the modern equivalent of a kingdom) is no different. Every business that exists as you read these words will one day no longer exist. GE is the only company left from the original Dow. It, too, one day will die. Like the American singer-songwriter and poet Jim Morrison said, "No one here gets out alive."[6]

No one.

This is why, perhaps, one of the traditional Buddhist preliminary practices is a meditation on death—to the point that one sutra says of all mindfulness practices, the meditation on death is "supreme." Why? As Tibetan Buddhists say, meditating on and having a familiarity with one's own death is extremely beneficial for a number of reasons.[7] If you have an awareness of your death, so the teachings go, you'll begin to recognize the urgency of your time here, and your days will become purposeful. As well, having an awareness of one's mortality tends to reorient one's priorities to something more pro-social.

There's a deep-rooted reason why titans like Bill Gates turn themselves to helping the world after they have mastered an industry (that reintegration we reviewed in chapter two). Time, which we all belong to whether we admit it or not, is the scarcest resource. This is why, as we discussed in chapter three, respecting others' time is the basis of partnership. When we realize, not as an intellectual construct but as an emotional conviction, that our time here is finite, we will act purposefully.

A sense of purpose is vision.

At its root, vision is ineffable—it cannot be fully described in words. This is because vision is not wholly conceptual. Rather, it is also a feeling, a conviction, a sense. Perhaps the reason there's disagreement about what's a mission statement or a vision statement is due to the not totally linguistic nature of the purpose. Perhaps it's best to put it plainly. Vision is what we're to do with the time we have. And if we look at the central business theses of a few leading companies, we can see that they prioritize not only revenue—though surely that's essential—but also the purpose of the work that they do. And that purpose is critical to staying a long-term course.

Amazon: In Defense of the Long Term

With the passing of Steve Jobs, Jeff Bezos is now regarded as the most important CEO in consumer technology. He is vocal, experimental, and since his original shareholder letter in 1997, he has been a champion of long-term growth. Bezos has said that a business, at a fundamental level, is either aligned with customers or against them, and it is this customer alignment that is at the center of his long-termism. In his 2013 letter,

Bezos mentioned a comment made by *Slate* columnist Matthew Yglesias, who wrote that Amazon "is a charitable organization being run by elements of the investment community for the benefit of consumers." Bezos rejected the premise, contending that "delighting customers earns trust," a trust which forms a partnership between the user and the brand. This, Bezos said, allowed for more business down the line from those customers, potentially in new businesses. When you take a long-term view, he concluded, the interests of shareholders and customers aligned.[8]

How so? Just as having a sense of partnership between team members with an organization is crucial, a sense of partnership between brand and customer is the highest-functioning form of brand identification. Having trust in a person (or a brand) minimizes the cognitive overhead incurred during decision-making, allowing us to act more swiftly. As Bezos suggested, it's in a business's interest to become trustworthy to its customers. That's what all that delight gets you. In this way, Amazon is in a mode of continual courtship to woo its customers.

As the contrarian tone of the letters to investors suggested, though, Bezos was comfortable with eschewing the short-term validations of profit in favor of the long-term promise of partnership. And as *Verge* writer Tim Carmody observed, since Amazon has become "the Enemy" to a number of industries (think: book publishing), Bezos's commitment to customer experience insulated the company from drawing the collective ire so often associated with titanic companies. "If Amazon is a victor," Carmody observes, "it must be a benevolent victor."[9]

Nike

Back in 2001, Phil Knight wanted Nike to have a new mission statement. The previous slogan: "To be the No. 1 sports-and-fitness company in the world." And what did now-CEO Mark Parker, who was then co-president, suggest?[10]

"To bring inspiration and innovation to every athlete* in the world.

*If you have a body, you are an athlete."[11]

It's as subtle as it is potent as it is expressive. Throughout its history, Nike has shown itself to be a company that not only can produce tremendous profits but can also exert a tremendous influence on culture. Back in the 1970s, it single-handedly made jogging a part of American life. During the course of its existence, Nike has helped bring mainstream fitness and its track-and-field ethos of training to broader culture. As a brand, Nike is not only deeply aspirational but also democratic—both principles are reflected in its mission statement.

IKEA

The IKEA business idea is to offer a wide range of home furnishings with good design and function at prices so low that as many people as possible will be able to afford them.[12]

There's something beautiful about referring to the central thesis of an enterprise as a "business idea." There's a lightness to it that isn't present when we talk about mission or vision statements. As well, here IKEA demonstrates its democratizing mission, a polite manifesto of bringing design to the people. Most of the time, beautifully designed home furnishings are created for the few who can afford them. From the beginning, IKEA has taken a different path. They have decided to side with the many.

As IKEA describes, its business idea is also its greatest differentiating factor. While the word "design" is usually associated with the elite few, IKEA has made it its mission to democratize a discipline that previously remained aspirational for many. And the company's emphasis on frugality and simplicity radiated from its leadership. Founder Ingvar Kamprad, though he was worth $42 billion, flew JetBlue and rode second class on trains. Siding with the many is evident in what Bill Moggridge, the director of the Cooper-Hewitt Design Museum, called its aesthetic of "global functional minimalism." In a profile of the company, *New Yorker* writer Lauren Collins described IKEA as "the invisible designer of domestic life, not only reflecting but also molding, in its ubiquity, our routines and our attitudes."[13] As well, IKEA's "many" is truly many. It has more than 300 stores in nearly forty countries, and in 2012 made more than $4 billion in profit.[14] Such is the power of siding with the many, partnering with the people.

Shadoka

The vision statement for my company, Shadoka, is this: "We accelerate sustainable growth." The Bengali word *shadoka* is derived from the Sanskrit word *sādhaka*. A *sādhaka* is a practitioner of a particular *sādhanā*. A *sādhaka*, or practitioner, is one who skillfully applies mind and intelligence in practice towards a goal. The Sanskrit word *sādhanā* literally translates to "a means of accomplishing something."

Accelerate sustainable growth: the combination of these three words deserves some discussion.

Acceleration is an increase in velocity. When we think about velocity, we think about rapidity, and with that speed comes a sense of the short term. After all, a sprint (the fastest form of running) predicts a race will be over quickly. A marathon, with its slow, enduring pace, lasts for hours. But here, acceleration is coupled with a counterpoint to that thinking—sustainable. If something sustains, it continues. The word comes from the Latin for "hold under." And then growth rather than profit. Living things grow. Taken together, "accelerating sustainable growth" means acting as a catalyst for our partners and customers to thrive. What's crucial, then, is to understand the nature of that catalyzation.

Everything connects. Making connections between disparate things is a key to creative thinking. Seeing these relationships is one of the keys to catalyzation. When we recognize the constellation of relationships within a group—like in an organization—we can begin to understand their shared alignment, a process that can be described as convergence.

By founding Shadoka, I wanted to create a company that would act as a vanguard and advocate of convergence, helping other organizations see the interdependencies within them and how they can better act in concert. To that end, we have developed in ourselves core assets of knowledge capital, understanding of what does and doesn't work for the long term within an organization, and then productized that understanding in the form of software platforms and more.

These assets aid entrepreneurs, management teams, and investors in improving their odds of long-term success by maximizing long-term quantitative and qualitative value for them and the ecosystems they serve (topics we'll return to throughout this book). The ultimate objective is to produce a wealth of new ideas, dynamic innovation, and sustainable opportunities. Financial success is a byproduct of what we do and what our customers do.

Vision produces a kind of organizational mindfulness. When you have a firm idea of what your priorities are and where you wish to go, you can reflect at the end of the day, month, and quarter to see if you are moving in accordance with that overarching quest.

FINDING THE PLATFORMS THAT ARE ALREADY THERE

Let's extend the metaphysical discussion from earlier. If vision is an expression of the soul of an organization, then platform is its body, the assets, whether internal or external, that lend the company its capabilities and character. We often call these "core competencies," which tend to grow organically in order to find solutions to problems. Whether an organization (or an individual) recognizes it in themselves, these competencies are platforms or assets with business applications.

Platform generation is taking assets that have already been created and finding new ways to use them. Think about the evolving business model of a nonfiction writer. They are taking the core assets of understanding and articulation and finding new ways to productize them. Annie Murphy Paul, who authors her weekly newsletter *The Brilliant Report*, writes about learning for *Time*, CNN, and *Psychology Today*. She describes herself as an author, journalist, consultant, and speaker.[15] That's a breadth of revenue streams from a specialized core asset, an understanding of learning. Platforms can, of course, also be tangible things. Automobile companies will use the same engine in a range of cars and, at times, provide engines for other manufacturers, bringing in more capital from a preexisting product. Similarly, if we are going to sustainably grow, we must reach limbs out into new markets in the same way a tree searches for sunlight.

UPS, the shipping giant, provides an interesting case study. According to *Harvard Business Review*, back in the mid-1990s, then-CEO Oz Nelson realized that the shipping industry was maturing and that growth rates would be slowing. It was time to find new opportunities for expansion—what we're referring to here as new growth platforms.[16]

A senior team led by Mike Askew (who would become CEO) did a thorough self-inquiry of what UPS was, similar to the soul-searching that IDEO prompted the Mayo Clinic to undertake. The team knew that UPS delivered packages, that much was apparent. But it was also a technology company, an insurance company, and an airline—the ninth-largest in the world. Its platform also came in the form of knowledge: the capabilities and know-how that they'd developed in order to be a leading shipping company.

What was the conclusion? To become its shipping best, the company developed excellence in operations, planning networks, and managing global infrastructure. Armed with that self-knowledge of possible platforms,

UPS was able to spot the needs its skill sets could fill, like when a customer came to them with a dilemma.

A major PC manufacturer needed help. Its customer service departments had to regularly send out hardware to users with rapid speed: two-day, next-day, same-day. It added up to a logistical knot. The manufacturer had ten shipping centers between North America, Europe, and Canada, all while managing stock, transfers, and returns. This was beyond its capabilities—but not for UPS. From the expertise UPS built as a shipping company, it had the knowledge to adroitly handle the flow of goods that left the manufacturer otherwise overwhelmed. UPS had the knowledge of themselves—and of the world—to allow them to untie their customer's knot, making for a primary example of holistic, interconnected thinking.

Seeing this vessel filled, Askew's team saw a new platform of growth for UPS. The shipping company could take its logistical expertise and source it out to customers, helping them to manage the flow of goods. And so, a new branch of UPS sprouted up: Service Parts Logistics—which soon became a core business for UPS. Such is the power of organizational mindfulness. Whether you're a regular person or a shipping company, having awareness of the phenomena happening inside and outside of you allows you to clearly see where you can connect with the world.

This has applications in the way we develop our professional lives as well, as the consideration of transferable skills is a key part of developing one's career. Bob Pozen, the finance-and-productivity expert mentioned previously, has what he calls "step-by-step optionality." With every job you take, you develop the skills that will avail you of the greatest number of future opportunities. (Management skills, for instance, are in constant demand, so it's wise to develop them, while the ability to pen a fine sonnet has a less stable demand curve.) For both organizations and individuals, we cannot know precisely what will be in demand in a decade. However, by paying close attention to trends in society and to the competencies we develop in ourselves and in our organizations, we can prime ourselves to act mindfully when opportunities present themselves.

In understanding platforms, we appreciate the wealth of possible intersections between ourselves, our organizations, and the world. In the same way that mindfulness meditation is not just awareness of one's breath but awareness of one's surroundings, organizational mindfulness does not end at the ever-blurring borders of the company but extends into the environments that they inhabit.

PLATFORMS CONNECT WITH ECOSYSTEMS

There's another beautiful old Indian story that can help us to understand the phenomena of our present world: *Indra's net*. In the Hindu tradition, Indra is the leader of the *devas*, or gods. He lives in heaven, atop Mount Meru, the center of the universe. Above his house was an infinite net of jewels, stretching out in all directions, each jewel glittering like a spider's web filled with morning dew. And if you were to look at any single one of these jewels, you would find the reflection of all the others in that single stone. The collective is reflected in the individual.

Just as our story of the elephant from earlier has many meanings—and illustrates the necessity of togetherness—so too does this bejeweled net. The all is reflected in the one. Students of capitalism know this well. The Foundation for Economic Education founder Leonard E. Read's beautiful essay "I, Pencil" provides a searching "autobiographical" account of our everyday writing instrument. He, speaking from the perspective of the pencil, declares that "not a single person on the face of this earth knows how to make me."[17] The pencil, so considered, is another symbol of interdependence. From a California cedar to Ceylon graphite, from the castor beans of its lacquer to the rapeseed oil of its *factice* (that is, the eraser), many parts come together to form the whole. Another meditation on product interdependence was recently written—independently of the first—by Kevin Ashton, technologist and coiner of the phrase "Internet of Things."

Writing for *Medium*, Ashton traces the chain of origination for the humble Coca-Cola can, a simple product he describes as "incomprehensibly complex." He traces the sourcing and processing of aluminum from Australia, vanilla extracted from dried Mexican orchids, coca leaves from South America, and chemical additives like carbon dioxide gas and phosphoric acid. This tool chain, Ashton writes, produces seventy million cans of Coke a day, available for purchase for a handful of change on street corners across the planet. That can, he says, is a product of the whole planet, showing not only chains of tools but chains of minds combining across time and space. Coke is a drinkable symbol of interconnectedness. The "famously American product is not American at all," he says.[18]

If we unpack this further, we can see the reciprocal indebtedness inherent to innovation and process. All of these processes, from the agricultural skills of harvesting and drying vanilla to the processing of heating phosphate rock and turning it into phosphorous, are taught and learned by students and teachers. When we allow for a deep appreciation to grow around the objects we interact with—including the book or device you're reading now—you begin to become sensitive to how our individual lives and the individual products we sell are deeply shared endeavors. This is what we're talking about when we talk about ecosystems. People, organizations, and products are obviously or subtly connected. As organizations, what we're connecting with is the ecosystem. Platform finding is seeking out the nooks and crannies of the market where our capabilities thrive and then meeting needs in new ways.

James F. Moore was the first to apply ecosystem to a business context. He wrote that a business ecosystem was "an economic community supported by a foundation of interacting organizations and individuals."[19]

These ecosystems, he wrote, encourage companies to coevolve their capabilities. This comes in several flavors.

Sometimes an ecosystem can sprout up around a product, like the range of cases, headphones, and other paraphernalia that surround the iPhone and iPad. As well, a company can sprout whole economic worlds, as was the case of the App Store. And in that case, the App Store itself was a new platform for Apple. Amazon also sprouted ecosystems from new business platforms. For example, Marketplace, from which third-party vendors—who in an early age would be considered competitors—can offer their wares on Amazon, creating an ecosystem in and of itself.

In a very similar sense, ecosystem thinking has become a cornerstone of web publishing. The broad swathe of unpaid contributors creating content for HuffPost, BuzzFeed, and other publishing platforms do so in exchange for growing their individual readership and brand. And Amazon has grown an ecosystem in publishing as well. Its Kindle store is both closed and proprietary, lending the company a breadth of authors and publishers who create value for themselves as well as Amazon with their work.

Why are ecosystems—and understanding them—crucial to sustainable innovation? They are the structure that surrounds and supports our businesses. They spread stakeholder-ship out from the business and into society. Ecosystem, then, is another way of saying partnership, a prism that lets us see the separate stars of the business sky as shared constellations. By having a deep awareness of the interdependence of our businesses, we can better improve them. That is the work of supply chain management and other logistical crafts. And when we press the premises of ecosystem thinking, we see an interdependence happening along many axes.

Think about a Kindle reader. Its material parts were sourced from around the planet, manufactured across Asia, and then sold all over the world, with reading material supplied from the world of publishing. All of those stakeholders contributed to the device owner's reading experience—and value was created up and down the chain.

TAKEAWAYS

We work for the long term. We do not eat the marshmallow right away; we devise strategies to create greater wealth for ourselves down the line. That overarching strategy is vision—often distilled into a single statement or idea—that acts as a guiding ethos for the company.

The long term is fluid. As our business grows, we have abiding attention on the breath of our workflow—the processes and core competencies that we develop to meet the needs of our constituents. And in paying attention to our customers and the broader environments, we can find opportunities to grow new platforms, taking advantage of the assets and skill sets already present within the organization.

The long term is interconnected. The reality we have at present is made up of constellations of causation value chains. Attending to this causation allows us to improve the lives of our customers and our employees, as we'll discuss in the next section.

PART TWO

PART TWO

PERSONAL EXPERIENCES, SHARED CULTURES, AND OTHER RHYTHMS

IN THE FIRST SECTION of our journey, we set out to map the fractious, fluid landscape of this world we're encountering. We have seen that all products, services, organizations, and persons perish—some more quickly than others. We have acknowledged that the prevailing punctuation of the innovation economy is the explosion, particularly those that drop mighty industries and organizations with a disruptive crash. But we have also learned that in such a setting of constant upheaval, a wise organization can not only thrive but also make an impact on the world at a velocity previously unknown. Opportunity and risk are two sides of the same coin. We love both.

Strangely, it's this love and appreciation stuff that is so integral to doing adaptive, innovative work. As revealed in the second chapter, before you can form healthy, productive, mutually reinforcing relationships with colleagues, customers, or anyone else, you must have such a relationship with yourself. This entails acknowledging what you do and don't know, what you can and can't feel, and where you have been and won't go. We've also established the absolute necessity of recruiting others to our cause— for our ignorance can only be informed by another's experience. As well, we've realized the counterintuitive truth that since our enterprises are impermanent, we must plan for the long term.

Having formed this foundation, we move to the crucial next section of our odyssey. Here the rubber of our so-called understanding will meet the road of our often-un-understandable realities. In our fifth chapter, we will examine how the handed-down methods of structuring an organization prevent it from doing its work (and how to fix that). In our sixth chapter, we'll examine how the handed-down methods of organizing people prevent them from doing their work (and how to fix that). Then, in the seventh chapter, we will see what a leader can do to bring together a flourishing culture where people are engaged in a shared endeavor to make the world better, whatever corner of the world they may be in.

So, let's share this endeavor.

CHAPTER 5

STRUCTURES OF INNOVATION

"Every man is a piece of the continent."
—*John Donne*[1]

YOU'RE SITTING ACROSS THE table from someone you just met, a clever, articulate, appreciative, and gracious person. You realize that the two of you went to similar schools, played the same sports, and enjoyed the same books. *It's going great,* you think to yourself. You're really hitting it off. You could even travel together—being stuck in an airport wouldn't be quite so awful if you were with this person.

Is this a date? Or is it a job interview?

Hard to tell the difference.

And the research of Lauren Rivera, associate professor at Northwestern's Kellogg School of Management, suggests that people making hires often confuse one with the other.[2]

It's counterintuitively intuitive. If you're hiring someone and your organization doesn't have an explicit rubric of merit, you'll use your own criteria. You'll define merit in your own way, which is probably using yourself as a rubric. For example, if you had similar educations, extracurriculars, and hometowns, or maybe you just click with them—isn't that reason enough to make a hire?

Often that's the case. At least in the consultancies, investment banks, and law firms that Rivera researched. Consciously or not, these firms have developed a process of cultural matching, in which companies replicate themselves because the people they hire share the same cultural characteristics. How's that work? When you're looking to hire someone based on an ambiguous notion of "merit"—and the merit is based on being like you—you're going to end up hiring someone deeply like yourself, even if they're of a different gender or ethnicity.

"There's an assumption that if you're different in sex or race or nationality, you'll bring different ideas to the table," she said to us in an interview. "But if you look at people who get into the firm, you're screening on people who participated in varsity athletics in one of ten schools, almost all your firm comes from one of three ZIP codes in the country, there's a lot of diversity [left] to be harnessed."[3]

Why does this matter? First, there's the humanistic, democratic ideal that progress is measured by more people being able to reach their fullest potential. But even if we didn't care for humanity, we'd have to recognize that diversity is a predictor of innovation. In conversation, Rivera made a Meyers-Briggs example. If you find that ENFPs are the ideal workers and hire a bunch of them, you're going to miss out on developing a project made for ENTJs. In other words, the less diverse an organization is—whether in the sense of race, class, gender, or personality type—the less it can empathize with the people outside of it, and the fewer partnerships it can form.

We are not the first to make such an argument. In an essay published in *Fortune*, Warren Buffett argued that since 1776, America had accomplished great things operating at only half capacity, as the country didn't include women in the economy. If women did insist on working, the Sage of Omaha noted, they would be limited to the noble professions of teaching, nursing, or secretarial positions, but little beyond that.[4]

This is not a new argument. It was first popularized by John Stuart Mill, a principal thinker in the British Enlightenment. He was a utilitarian philosopher who thought that the just action was the one that created the most benefit for the most people. Relatedly, he introduced the Marketplace of Ideas. Just as an open economy has a marketplace of goods—readily apparent from the souk to the farmers market—there's a similar though less tangible market of ideas available to choose from. The finest markets of goods are the ones that provide the widest selection.

That's obvious from the growth of Sears, the birth of the shopping mall, and the rise of Amazon. Similarly, a society will offer the best "products"—ideas, opportunities, and ways of life—when it includes the widest selection of ideas coming from the widest selection of suppliers.

In the way that a souk has products and a university has ideas, an organization is a similar collective. If we are indeed in the innovation economy, if indeed the uncovering of new, disruptive products and processes is as important as the optimization of existing ones, then we are incentivized to make our organizations as prone to innovation as possible. The more varied the backgrounds that contribute to that organizational marketplace, the greater the capacity for cross-pollination within the organization, and the greater the empathy we will have across cohorts of potential users. As we discussed in the previous chapter, organizations need to make themselves continually available to new business platforms, implying that the needed capacities within a team will remain somewhat latent, like seeds waiting for the right market conditions to sprout.

Yet, even if we accept that diversity predicts innovation, we might not act in accordance with that understanding. The way we conflate hiring and dating is evidence of our blind spots. During the unexamined experience of the interview, we get positive feedback from the engaging conversation and the validation that comes with sharing interests. It's intuitive to want to reward the person we've clicked with, especially if we're going to be spending untold hours and unseen flight delays together. (Though that may be a decision born of individual rather than organizational interest.) What's more, the replicating that follows hiring someone who shares all your interests hems in the diversity and, thus, the market for new ideas. Yet, it feels so natural to reward someone who we click with.

Knowing that unhealthy trends like firm replication can happen unconsciously, that they can even feel like the "natural" thing to do, warns us of the importance of vigilance in regarding the way that we work. The "usual" in business-as-usual needs to be examined and, if necessary, acted upon. In this particular case, the replication problem arose partially because people defaulted to "they're like me" in their validation process rather than following an established, rigorous rubric. Part of the solution is to usher more of the implicit action of the hiring process into explicit prescriptions. As well, Rivera suggests turning that hiring process into something quantifiable, rating each candidate across a range of skills and then tracking that performance over time. In this way, the process can become more systematized and repeatable. Though, as we'll see later, such systems must be re-examined as well.

As we discussed in the second chapter, a person can plot a more informed trajectory after inquiring into one's identity. This is also true of organizations, as we expanded on in the last chapter. But just as one must become intimate with one's mind and body in the path of growth, the organization must know not only its motivations and goals but also its structure. For, as we shall see, the structure of an organization predicts the products it creates. Architecture, then, is the topic of this chapter.

CONWAY'S LAW AND YAMMER

Melvin Conway was an early computer scientist. In 1967, he submitted a prescient essay to *Harvard Business Review*; it was a paper called "How Do Committees Invent?" The paper was rejected. In a blog post on the subject, Conway says that it was on the grounds that he did not prove his thesis. He then submitted the paper to an IT magazine called *Datamation*, where it saw publication in 1968. The paper is fascinating to us for the theory that it represents. It provides a crucial bridge between management and product, between groups of people and the things they make. Condensed for clarity, the thesis is as follows:

> "Any organization that designs a system . . . will inevitably produce a design whose structure is a copy of the organization's communication structure."[5]

Reflection

In other, more grandiose words, we can restate Conway's Law as saying that companies are destined to produce products that mirror their organizational structure. Or, even more extremely and poetically, we could simply say that the organization implies the product or that the organization is the product.

How can we get to such lofty claims? When we think of product, we tend to think of a single, static event or item: a magazine is released in an issue, a mop is delivered to a store, and a doctor sees a patient. But now that every industry is pressured to release more and more products, we have more physical touch points with the people interacting with them. Beyond that, the social web has brought us to a point where humans on either side of the divide between organization and user are continuously conversing with one another (and, as in any good conversation, listening deeply).

And it's perhaps most obvious in cases of software and the culture of iteration that has grown up around the social web. Customers are continually signaling what they do and do not want. Companies are responding to those spoken or measured needs as quickly and effectively as they can. It's as though the people inside the organization and the people outside the organization are throwing a ball back and forth, and that ball is the product. The customer is interacting with the organization as much as it is the product, which is why the organization and its structure should be as accommodating and responsive as the product itself.

Blockbuster, Yammer, and Petrified Organizations

It's become a truism that we live in an age of disruption. Incumbent companies become outmoded, outstripped, and outperformed by younger companies. Why? The canonical causation is that the insurgents provide a product at a much lower cost than the incumbents. But, as Adam Pisoni, the chief technology officer of Yammer (a social enterprise company), said to us, disruption may have its roots in organizational structure.[6]

He uses a now-classic example: the entwined fates of Netflix and Blockbuster. Blockbuster, as American readers of a certain age will remember, was a video rental service that allowed people to watch movies at home. The medium by which it delivered that value? Physical storage, in the form of video cassettes and, later, DVDs. As Pisoni observes, Blockbuster was built around that physical storage.

"They couldn't change," Pisoni says, "because all they could think about was how to improve the thing they did, not the value they offered."

In this way, Blockbuster's organizational entrenchment made itself brittle. Pisoni says it organized itself around the way—or the medium—it provided value, not the value that it created for the customer. Job descriptions, organizational structures, and the like were built around making video rental stores, not helping people to watch movies. And when that gap between medium and value opens up, Pisoni says, disruption happens. If there's a ghost of a video rental store in the neighborhood, you'll know what he means.

As Pisoni argues, and as Schumpeter portended last century, the pace of these radical changes has accelerated. Fifty years ago, paradigm shifts like the ones that did Blockbuster in—the mainstreaming of the internet, then broadband access, and the increasingly streaming nature of video—would have come over the course of decades or longer. When the pace of change is that slow, optimizing for predictable efficiency is a sensible model, since the operating context remains reasonably stable. But when the rate of paradigm change increases, like when people move from desktops to laptops to smartphones to tablets in turns of five or so years, building a rigidly efficient system is no longer fitting.

"Suddenly, focusing on efficiency and predictability becomes detrimental. Focusing on organizing on value or agility becomes the only game in town," Pisoni continued. "We've clearly crossed the Rubicon where the old, traditional structured companies are no longer effective."

Founded in 2008, Yammer has emerged as a leader—if not the leader—of enterprise social networks. Founded by Pisoni and David O. Sacks, the startup grew quickly, eventually raising $142 million in funding. In June 2012, Microsoft acquired them for $1.2 billion, and some serious cross-pollination is occurring. (Microsoft Office, from what Pisoni says, is integrating with Yammer.) This means that work is getting more social. But we are more interested in the way that Yammer itself works.

"You have to understand Yammer is a product which was built to make companies better companies," Pisoni says. "That puts the lens back on us."

Yammer realized that it was great at iterating its product, cranking out new versions, and measuring in varied metrics. Then it decided to turn that ethos inward. Why didn't the organization become something to be iterated on, to rapidly test each version for efficacy? So, it did.

"We created a culture of organizational iteration where it gave us room to experiment and fail because everybody from employees to managers knew this is just a big experiment," Pisoni says. "Nothing's permanent, and anyone can suggest any changes. It's everyone's responsibility to think about the system, not just their jobs."

What does that look like? You'll find in Yammer's San Francisco offices the engineering team has something it calls "The Big Board." Products are listed on one side, and their teams are listed on the right. These teams are reassigned in a weekly meeting.

Yes, they have an org chart, but instead of being organized by products and processes, it's organized by skill set. And your boss doesn't tell you what to do.

They pull people out of the org chart and make a temporal team. One of the engineers is made tech lead, and that person runs that project. They'll be your boss for two to ten weeks, which gives upper management a chance to see who makes for a good manager. Instead of people working on single projects for years and getting attached to them, they get moved around, removing ego-clinging to the project and focusing on the outcome.

This ephemeral team strategy is applicable to domains beyond enterprise startups. Viewing disruption as a product of companies becoming brittle suggests that we would be served by loosening the vice-like grip we currently have on job descriptions. Not that we no longer need them, but we must recognize that a person's potential contributions extend beyond what's printed on their business card.

Yammer has, in essence, created an environment with a swarm of ephemeral startups.

Since Yammer's structure is so fluid, Pisoni says, they can keep growing—they're at 200 workers in R&D alone now—and not slow down.

In so doing, Yammer has developed a loose, organic, rotational, rapidly reincarnating structure for itself. One of the benefits of the rotationality, Pisoni says, is that you get implicit knowledge sharing. Why is this so crucial? Since problems are emergent, the best practices for dealing with them are equally emergent. There isn't a playbook written from on high that tells you what to do in this or that situation. Rather, it's your network—the people you can call upon, the institutional knowledge you can summon, partnerships you have—that's your playbook. And the more that people are interwoven with others in the work they do, the better decisions they can make, the more trust people can have with each other, and the faster they can move. The faster you move, the faster you can produce a new version, the faster you can get feedback, the faster you can improve. The faster you can adapt to providing the value that customers are looking at your brand for, the faster you gain their trust. In this way, the partnerships that develop within an organization shape the partnership between the organization and its users, customers, and constituents.

This is precisely why we need to tend to our team's networks.

Connectivity Predicts Success

How crucial are your at-work relationships? Larry Miller is a medical statistician and a cofounder of Activate Networks, a consultancy that incorporates advances in network science to understand how companies work—and how the relationships within them drive success.[7]

Activate Networks was recently called in to a large, innovation-centric engineering firm, the kind with thousands of engineers in a given plant, half a dozen or so people to a team, all with the primary job of dreaming up new products. To get a read on how innovation happened, Miller and his team mapped the network of individuals in the organization, then mapped the prescribed metrics for success (like leading to a patent or bringing something to the commercial marketplace) and superimposed those successes onto the network of engineers.

What Miller found was striking. Aside from years of experience, the highest correlation for success metrics was successful relationships. And not for the team as a whole, but whether or not a team had an individual who was highly connected to the total network. If you're working in a closet somewhere, Miller says, it doesn't matter how great your work is.

What makes for a powerful network for an individual? Miller says that you need to have broad connections. The highest performers tend to have cross-departmental links, meaning that if all of your primary connections are in your own department, you won't be as effective. As well, you don't want to only have connections on your level of the hierarchy, but both up and down the ladder. He's careful to note it's not merely that you have as many connections as possible; it's about the strength of those connections. When you're onboarding employees, setting cross-departmental connections will be of benefit to each individual but also each team.

The reason these teams with more connected individuals were successful is because they could spread their ideas throughout their organization, gather feedback on those ideas, and gain support for them. There's something deeply intuitive about that. If you go to a strong connection of yours looking for commentary on your project and they give commentary, there's a sense of mutual investment, a sense of partnership that will develop from truly constructive criticism. At an emotional level, there's a growth of co-investment; at a conceptual level, your and their ideas get shaped and recombined. Whether or not you have a blindfold on, you're getting more hands on the elephant.

We can think of the quality of the relationship as the bandwidth through which knowledge can move. If you work with someone but do not trust them, you will not be able to exploit the implicit knowledge sharing that a rotational architecture like Yammer's is built to promote. And as the Activate Networks example shows, teams within the engineering firm found success when at least one person was connected with the rest of the organization, allowing the insights of the team to gain exposure and feedback from other groups, disciplines, and perspectives within an organization. But if you don't have high-bandwidth relationships with people, you won't be able to develop that same sense of mutual buy-in.

As Yammer evidences, network building isn't the province only of the outrageously social or the relentlessly networking. Since connections are so indicative of the success of projects, organizations can take care to increase the quantity and quality of relationships inside them. Think of a person's experiences as granting them a certain amount of surface area. If you want your organization to be expansive, you need to have overlap, but you also need portions of each individual team member to be unreplicated anywhere else. In this way, the uniqueness of the individual informs the uniqueness of the organization. Getting people from diverse disciplines and work histories to work together is one of the best ways to architect innovation—a clustering we'll discuss later in the chapter.

THE ORGANIZATIONAL OPPORTUNITIES OF MATURE COMPANIES

But structural innovation isn't only for scrappy startups. Mature companies have unique opportunities of their own. The breadth and depth of large organizations lend them to intersectional innovations. You can also call this combinatorial creativity: what happens when two previously unconnected ideas reveal their relatedness.

This is a phenomenon often found in art. When Japan relaxed its isolationism in the late 19th century, the wealth of its culture pollinated across the world. Art historians will tell you how the flowers ornamenting the backgrounds of Van Gogh's portraits came from the postcards of Japanese art that the Dutchman collected, same as the nontraditional, diagonal compositions that marked his later work. But this cross-pollination accelerates not only the growth of painting but of products. P&G is a perfect example.

The Many Intersections of Procter & Gamble

When A. G. Lafley became CEO at P&G in June 2000, the company was falling apart. His predecessor, Durk Jager, had just been thrown out after seventeen months of missing earnings projections, and as *Business Week* notes, its stock dropped $7 during his first week on the job. By the end of the year, the company had lost a total of $85 billion in market capitalization. To dig itself out of that hole, they sold off failing brands—Crisco, Jif, and Folgers, to name a few.[8] But beyond getting trimmer, P&G became better connected.

This again extends mindfulness—an awareness of what's happening inside and outside a body—to an organizational level by seeing what assets, already present in an organization, can combine and meet the market in new ways. Since gigantic corporations like P&G have a wide set of businesses, the potential for combining competencies is far greater than its smaller peers. Its work runs across verticals, meaning you can make novel combinations within the organization, bringing new products and product lines to market.

Crest's transition from dental care to oral care is a telling example. Back in 2000, it was all toothpaste and toothbrushes. But in his 2008 book *The Game Changer*, Lafley reveals how Crest grew.[9] He writes of the Corporate Innovation Fund within P&G, essentially the corporation's in-house venture capitalist fund. That fund provided for a combination of talents and technology between different arms of the company, one of which resulted in Crest Whitestrips.

P&G CTO Bruce Brown would later unpack the cross-pollinating logic in an interview with *Forbes*:[10]

> "Often [the] connection of seemingly disparate technologies delivers disruptive ideas. The magic in a big company is how to create space for connections, so an idea person can bump into a technology person," he says, citing Whitestrips as an example of the power of intersectional thinking. The film came from packaging in their paper products, the bleach from their fabric products, and the glue from another application, he says, combining for "a novel product delivering a service you could previously only get professionally," he said, "but now get at home."

According to a *Harvard Business Review* article, the product faced some internal naysayers during its development. So, P&G brought in a general manager from the Swiffer sweeper product group to guide the idea into reality. As well, to win over dentists wary of endorsing themselves out of business, P&G made a Whitestrips Supreme product for dental office use.

The Whitestrips story is an interesting foil to the fall of Blockbuster. While as Yammer CTO Adam Pisoni observed that the video rental service had trapped itself within its sprawling structure to better produce a single product, P&G shows that large companies can exploit the existing structures of their businesses, so long as they keep an eye on creating a value that their customers want. P&G was, in fact, able to do some disruptive innovation itself. Crest's Whitestrips translated a high-end service into a customer's domestic setting. And to great reward. In their first year, Whitestrips generated $200 million in revenue and grabbed close to ninety percent of the market share.[11]

What the Whitestrips show—beyond a brighter smile—is the power of intersectional thinking. Taking the expertise between several departments and combining them will yield new ideas. That the home cleaning department and the oral care department would find a market-shaping collaboration is unexpected—which is precisely why such experimental, combinatorial strategies are so effective. But this isn't just something to be found in organizations. We as individuals can use it too.

To bring intersectional thinking into your day-to-day life, you could keep two books on your nightstand—one fiction and the other nonfiction, one contemporary and the other a classic—and then find the intersections. This is also, perhaps, one of the great joys of undergraduate learning. Since all academic traditions are studies of humans and the universe, they all have more to do with each other than their departments suggest. One will study perception in art history, cognitive science, and marketing classes, and the studies in one field will inform that of the other.

There's a social element, too. Lunch is as good a time as any to cultivate cross-pollination. Just as a city like New York or London benefits from the divergent histories that intersect there, you can make your lunch hour, perhaps once a week, an ephemeral city. Invite people from different disciplines in and outside of your organization for a meal and a conversation. When you invite someone to a meal, you invite all their experiences and ideas, too. Since we all have a different hand on the elephant, getting together allows us to compare notes on what this beast called working life is and let the insights arise from there.

ORGANIZING WITH TALENT CLUSTERS

Is there a way to organize for these sparks? We think so.

**Cluster: a loose, cross-functional method for
creating and implementing ideas**

What if you took Yammer's methodology of adaptability, rapidity, and impermanence for structuring their engineering team and moved it into a broader context? What if you made the synergy that P&G engineered to create Whitestrips more replicable? What if, instead of only trying to create a process within a piece of software or a new oral care product, the multi-talented team was planning an organization's future, meeting with users, or another project? You'd have a taut, time-bound collection of people assembled around a specific task. We call such a group a cluster: our way of systematizing the emergent processes of Yammer, P&G, and other innovators.

Clusters come into being to address a particular challenge and then disperse once that challenge is met. Though, as the Yammer example points out, the bonds that the individuals within those teams form remain. This is also a way of weaving together the total network of an organization, further allowing ideas and feedback to flow between pieces of the whole—the explicit links of the short-lived cluster form implicit, long-lived bonds between the people within them. And the trust that arises will accelerate the movement of the organization.

Think of a cluster as a leaner version of a committee, council, or circle. To wrap our minds around the cluster, let's evaluate what committees and their ilk are usually for: to map and oversee the responsibilities related to a given task, giving us (un)interesting terms like "steering committee," fancy ways of dictating to everyone what they are to do. But in the innovative, agile, and creative-based economy, people do best when they can steer themselves. A cluster is a way of cooperating with the fact that humans crave autonomy. It helps us organize people without encumbering them.

But this is not anarchy. Clusters inherit much of the structure of top-down hierarchies—accountability, reward systems, and measurement of performance are all present—while including bottom-up innovations. Those include recruiting the resources and personnel they need within or outside of the organization, an emphasis on self-direction, and aligning their actions to the vision of the whole. It's all of what you need, as an advertisement might say, and none of what you don't.

To distill, clusters have the following characteristics:

- **Tailored agenda:** Each cluster has a specific reason for existing, with an agenda of objectives that matches that purpose.

- **Time-bound existence:** Clusters emerge when needs arise. They disband when their objectives have been completed.

- **Evolving membership:** Membership to a cluster is not fixed but is fluid, with talent and perspectives changing to suit changing tasks.

- **Self-organizing responsibility:** Clusters develop their own structure and operational rules. They alone are responsible for their operation and its results.

- **Adaptive ethos:** The culture and personality of the cluster aligns with its purpose. Some are explorative, some are directed.

There are three primary types of clusters representing the three phases of development for a lifecycle of a product, process, or service. They are visioning, ecological, and implementation-oriented.

Visioning Cluster

How does a product begin? Like all living things, it must be conceived. This is the work of the visioning cluster. They sketch out the potentials of a product. This is more than a "leadership committee." Yes, managers should be involved, but it's also critical that implementation-focused and user-facing team members be involved. At this opening stage, it is crucial that the cluster has a diversity of perspectives within the organization. As Professor Rivera reminds us, if a product is going to be aimed at a range of cohorts, those cohorts need to be represented in the visioning cluster.

The idea here is to take down the velvet rope surrounding "leadership." Often "leadership" is a euphemism for the people that make the most money in an organization, which places the cart before the horse. Rather, leadership, as we noted in chapter one, is a way of owning the impact that you or your organization is going to have upon the world. This demands foresight of what's to come and insight into how to get there—which is not necessarily reliant on the amount of money you make. Indeed, as we've noted before, if you only have wealthy people making decisions for an organization that has more than just wealthy people in it, you'll be blinding your perspective. You'll have the same hands on the elephant.

Instead, bring people with leadership qualities into the visioning cluster. It's healthy to have a range of experience levels included, since that will create intergenerational bonds within the organization and illuminate blind spots.

Ecosystem Cluster

Bringing a product to market is intensely interdependent, relying on suppliers, customers, intermediaries, and partners to make it happen. The ecological cluster's primary purpose is to connect with these varied players within the ecosystem, building support across all these spheres.

As Dave Gray observes in *The Connected Company*, a fundamental characteristic of our area is that the line between organization and customer is increasingly perforated; that is, people outside an organization are increasingly being represented and included within.[12] These ports of exchange are ecological clusters.

Ecological clusters can take many forms. It's assumed that consumer-facing organizations will have a person with social media responsibilities, but that is perhaps the immature model of the ecological cluster. The mature model goes further in including shareholders in decision-making. Suppliers and intermediaries may participate directly in the ecological clusters' functioning, though if there are parties who don't care to be involved, we can use a proxy, someone who can accurately represent their point of view.

While we cannot peer into the inner workings of P&G, we can surmise that something of the ecosystem cluster occurred when they put together the Crest Whitestrips, especially the advanced model for dental professionals. Sensing that the disruptive product would harm preexisting relationships, P&G was canny to make the premium product to preserve those partnerships.

A theme that emerges again and again within contemporary life is the increasingly palpable interconnectedness of every organization's work. We're behooved, then, to have people on hand who can lend us the benefit of context. We want to have many perspectives on what the elephant in the room—our product—looks like. We'll go into detail about who in the next chapter.

Implementation Cluster

Ideas don't realize themselves. They need to be ushered into life by people. Just as the visioning cluster is composed of people that affect an idea's conception, the implementation cluster is composed of those tasked with instantiation. They get the work done, joining the prescribed vision with the context described by the ecological cluster.

Members of the implementation cluster are focused on making things. Its membership is more defined than the other clusters. It must contain every element necessary to bring the vision into reality. Like the other clusters, participation varies depending on the dynamics of the cluster. Unlike the other clusters, however, member roles and participation are dictated by the implementation processes.

The implementation process happens in three steps (which are less separate than the sequence suggests): prototyping, validating, and taking to market. This is a generalized process for whether you're building toasters, software, a health care workflow, or a solar panel. Visioning is concerned with the blueprinting of an idea in the look and feel of a product. A coffee cup, for instance, will have its initial idea and purpose, but its specifications will not start to be laid out until the implementation phase. In this way, the product lifecycle is a movement from vagueness to specificity. In the implementation phase, we start to get specific.

Prototyping is different from visioning in that you're actually starting to gather momentum for this product. If Leonardo da Vinci were making a cannon, he'd have to first test the cannon out, which would require gathering the physical materials and funding necessary in order to make the first mock-up. The prototyping phase is simply minimum product. Let's build our first cup of coffee, our first cannon, and our first piece of code, then start tinkering with it.

Next is the validation phase. You could think of this as a mature prototype you're testing in more contexts. Here is where the ecosystem cluster plays a crucial role. As we know, the success of every product is contingent upon a staggering number of factors, and an organization cannot know all of those factors as they prototype. We end up learning things like we're in a dark hotel room by stumbling over furniture while pawing after the light switch. This is the part where you stub your toe and whack your shin. But in the validating phase, you're still in a controlled, pre-release situation. This allows us to fail small, fail often, and improve rapidly. It's important to note that some products never make it out of the validation phase. If, for instance, a distribution partner backs out, it's better to find out in this phase and cancel the project than roll out a less-than-excellent product.

Then, after prototyping and validating comes the launch, the mass production. This has different stages of finality depending on the circumstance. If you're creating a physical product, it's not going to be modifiable once it's out in the world. But if you're building software or an organizational process, then you can edit the product much more readily. Of course, a launch isn't simply the physical creation of a product but the way it is welcomed into the world. This suggests that from the blueprinting phase on, all of these clusters, all of this blueprinting, needs to be integrated, taking into account how all of the people interacting with the product, from those within the organization to contingent partners to end users, need to be represented from the beginning. That process will emerge as we continue on.

TAKEAWAYS

What comes automatically may not be best for the organization. As evidenced by Lauren Rivera's research into the ways that elite firms hire, doing what comes naturally—like hiring people that you click with—can actually obstruct innovation. If you're not mindful of the culture that's being created, it will emerge thoughtlessly rather than by design.

Structures, when built unmindfully, can kill companies. Organizational structures are not inherently harmful. But they can wreck your organization if you rigidly cling to the product they're built to deliver rather than the value they attempt to create.

Structures, when used intelligently, can disrupt markets. But just as unmindful clinging to structures can choke off innovation, clever cross-pollination between groups can encourage it. As the story of Crest Whitestrips shows and the conception of the clusters suggests, this is a powerful tactic for finding new platforms. But this demands a culture of openness, regardless of an organization's size, which we'll dive deeply into over the next two chapters.

CHAPTER 6

PERFORMING INNOVATION

*"Acting is not about being someone different. It's finding the similarity
in what is apparently different, then finding myself in there."*
—Meryl Streep[1]

BACK IN 1978, A house in Sherman Oaks, California, hosted a storm
of brains that would shape the history of film. George Lucas, who had
just assembled a movie called *Star Wars*, and Steven Spielberg, who
had just done a flick called *Jaws*, met in a small house with the screenwriter
Lawrence Kasdan. And as a transcript of their talks featured on *The New
Yorker*'s website shows, in a handful of days, the three generated ideas for
their next movie, a 1930s-style adventure that would recapture the pulp-
style romps they grew up watching. What would they call it? Something
like *Indiana Smith*.[2]

In the course of the conversation, they banter about the hero they're
making. He's as intelligent as he is scruffy, equal parts Clark Gable and
Clint Eastwood. He's a "bounty hunter of antiquities," clad in khaki
pants, leather jacket, and felt hat. He's handy with a pistol but prefers the
bullwhip he keeps at his side. He's an accomplished professor with a bug
for adventure.

But what's most exciting about their conversation, as *The New Yorker* writer Patrick Radden Keefe observes, is the "voyeuristic thrill" of seeing two titans-on-the-make speak with unguarded enthusiasm. The kind of enthusiasm that encourages bad ideas.

From how the transcript reads, Lucas acts as a graceful leader, guiding the flow of Spielberg's creative energy. Spielberg volleys ideas for more character attributes—he's got a thing for ghosts, he's trained in Kung Fu, he's a great gambler. Lucas, rather than scoffing outright and shaming his enthusiastic conversation partner, says that "we might be stacking too much into this character," that the "thing of it is [that] it's good if we delineate a fairly clean personality so that it doesn't become too confused." He seems to have an implicit understanding of how our emotional states affect our creative output, and he is mindful of that in conversation.

But Spielberg's same boyish bursts beget some of the franchise's most memorable scenes, like when the idea for the film's opening action sequence erupts from Spielberg. Our hero heads into a cave, climbs up an inclined tunnel, and grabs the artifact he's seeking. Then, all of a sudden, a trap is sprung: "a sixty-five-foot boulder that's form-fitted to only roll down the corridor" comes right after him, and he has to race out, blocking the entrance to the cave. Our scruffy professor emerges unscathed, and the audience is enraptured. It's the most blockbuster of blockbuster scenes, and it burst out of the filmmaker whole.

In another instance, Spielberg describes a scene where Jones falls asleep on a small airplane and awakes to find himself in free fall and that everybody's parachuted away—a scene that would make it into *Temple of Doom*. Lucas, in his grace, pulls the idea out of him.

"He's trapped in this airplane, and it's going down," Spielberg says.

"Then what happens?" Lucas replies. "One sentence further, and it's a great idea."

———

We think this shows the magic of the creative process. Whether you're making feature films or features for a web app, these innovations can either arrive piece by piece or all at once. And this creative process, both in its initial sparks and conclusive movements, is very much affected by the way the people work with one another. If Lucas wouldn't have been so gently conducive to Spielberg's ideas, we may never have seen *Raiders of the Lost Ark*. If we are also in the business of making blockbusters—in whatever field that may be—we'd do well to learn how to work together in ways that maximize the creative potential of everyone involved.

Our discussion in this chapter is an expansion of that in the last. We previously laid out strengths built in the ephemeral teams of Yammer and the corporation-sized cross-pollination of P&G, combining those ideas into time-bound, goal-contingent teams we call clusters. Here, we will combine those clusters with knowledge assembled about how people do their best work—with a combination of freedom and rigor. In other words, this chapter will have two acts:

- First, we will discuss **the acting roles** that make up the various clusters. These are the roles that do the work.

- Second, we will consider **the rules** that hold the clusters together— the new ways of collaborating and working in a team, how we play the roles, and how we are measured.

THE ACTORS

In the same way an actor can have central dramatic strengths but play many characters, a team member can have a core skill set and contribute in many fashions. Recognizing that a role is a mask, filter, or persona to be tried on, we can work more fluidly and with greater fulfillment. This is the genesis of what we'll call the "acting role." To motivate us, let's take a look at the problems of the traditional system.

Role As Performance

In 1990, Judith Butler set off a theoretical bomb. The University of California, Berkeley, professor released *Gender Trouble*, a major (and controversial) work of feminist philosophy that had a hand in founding queer theory. In it, she introduces the concept of gender performativity—which is useful to understanding the way work works.

For Butler, gender is something constructed. That is, it is created by society and how people behave and engage within a society. It does not exist intrinsically within a person. To say that gender is performative means we've taken on a role and that the acting or role-playing that we're doing is central to our gender. In other words, we walk and speak and talk in ways to "consolidate an impression" of whatever gender we present to the world.

"We act as if being a man or being a woman is a true reality," she said in a recent interview, "[while] actually it's a phenomenon being produced all the time or reproduced all the time."[3]

If you don't consolidate the impressions of the gender that are accepted by your society, you may be in trouble. For Butler, gender is something that's "policed," most evident in the treatment of effeminate boys and masculine girls. That policing can take many forms, whether schoolyard bullying or psychiatric normalization. These gender norms, Butler says, do a violence.

What kind of violence? Since this is a humble business book, we can't make exhaustive arguments, but it seems clear that by performing a gender, it becomes a shell, prescriptively constricting the kind of role we have. As well, it feels deeply true that if a person is scolded, shunned, arrested, or otherwise penalized for expressing what feels deeply true to them— their concept of self and the way they present and express that self to the world—they would suffer the initial trauma of self-rejection that could fester into self-denial or self-hatred if they are not yet emotionally resilient. These are not healthy things. And we'll leave their explication to experts.

Do Butler's ideas inform the way we regard the workplace? Certainly. It's useful to think of workplace roles as performative—that is, there are certain accepted (and unaccepted) behaviors for managers, for salespeople, for designers, for technologists, etc. After all, wouldn't a computer programmer be looked at strangely in a meeting of designers? Or a customer service person in a huddle of managers? Would they not be better served by sticking to the confines of their predefined roles? We think not.

To understand why, let's look at another field. Lexicography, the art and science of composing dictionaries, supplies us with a useful vocabulary. Within that linguistically charged world, there are two primary camps: prescriptivists and descriptivists. The prescriptivists contend that the definition assigns the proper use of the word, while a descriptivist contends that the definition arises from the way a word is used. A hard prescriptivist cringes at the fact that "text" has become a verb in the age of the mobile phone, while a descriptivist would welcome the new use as an evolution of the language—a language that describes the world its speakers are interacting with. And do we really expect people to say, "send a text message to me" instead of "text me"? Probably not.

Similarly, we should be careful to identify job descriptions as just that, descriptions, not prescriptions. They tell you what has been done in the position, not everything you could do. This is why, perhaps, people get commended for "acting outside of their job description." They are acting outside the rigidity that a clung-to title would suggest.

Which brings us back to gender. Just as there is, outside of progressive societies, a brutalizing bias against people who fail to act according to gender roles, there is a less outright violent (but similarly inhibiting) bias that hangs over the heads of the people trapped in job prescriptions. Our guess is that was part of what undid Blockbuster, as Yammer CTO Adam Pisoni explained in the last chapter. If people feel like they'll be punished for acting outside of their roles—like if the designer starts acting like a developer, if a frontline worker meets with the managers—they won't. And that rigidity is the opposite of adaptation, the opposite of doing something new, and the opposite of innovation.

What does a less rigid but still rigorous form of organization look like?

Deciding on Your Role(s)

We think it looks like a cluster—the goal-driven, time-bound teams we described in the last chapter. But what's unique, what shifts us beyond the job prescriptions, is to recognize that the role a person has in a given project depends on the project. It neither defines nor inhibits their professional self. Just as there's a difference between a battle and a war, the role for a project is not the role for a career.

In other words, working in clusters acknowledges the deeply relative nature of a given project. There is the way you relate to the overall goal, the tasks within that goal set, and the way your work relates to that of your colleagues. Your place within the team is inspired by the assignment at hand and how you're applying your skills in that context. And once that context completes, your role does as well. It acknowledges that work is a performance. To borrow the vocabulary of theatre, what you're doing is playing.

You're playing a role in the same sense that actors in Elizabethan England were players. As Jaques reminds us in *As You Like It*, "All the world's a stage."[4] The cluster (and its project) is the drama at hand. The team members are the players. As in theatre, every drama has its own rules, its own logic, and its own structure. But before we get to that structuring, let's look at the *dramatis personae*.

As we stated above, the role is dependent upon the work at hand. A single person could have different roles in different clusters, perhaps in a single day. We are not alone in recognizing this inherent flexibility. In his *Ten Faces of Innovation*,[5] IDEO partner Tom Kelley draws out his various personas (also a theatrical term!). Lou Adler, the human resources expert, has been writing sound commentary on the subject as well.[6] For Kelley, we've entered into a "post-disciplinary world" in which people's work doesn't quite fit under "engineer," "marketer," or "project manager." We need a new vocabulary, Kelley and Adler contend.

And we agree. Since we're in this disruptive and disrupting working life, we need to optimize around the creation and implementation of new ideas. With that being the case, we've arrived in a place where the engineering of a product includes its designing and visioning. The ways in which we work need new definitions, though what they are (and perhaps have always been) are roles.

From what we can tell, there are four main roles. All of which are leading.

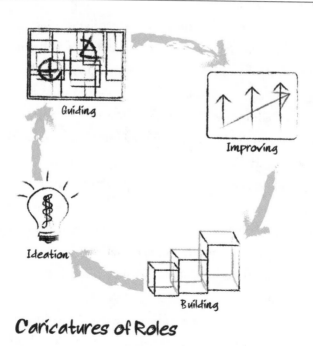

Caricatures of Roles

Ideation roles: dream up, discover, invent, and spread ideas

Guiding roles: manage, navigate, oversee, and develop ideas

Building roles: implement, execute, and finish turning ideas into processes

Improving roles: expand, reduce, and tinker with existing products and processes

Previously, we have discussed before the relationship between humility and curiosity. If you seek out knowledge from the world, your perceptions will naturally be bolstered and affected. But if you are uncurious about the world outside your own perception or your own organization, you will soon find yourself convinced of the rightness of your own way. (Like, say, Blockbuster.) The people that ensure an organization retains its inquisitive interest are the **ideation roles**—people studying the world and people around them, ferreting out what could be with a mixture of personal and organizational mindfulness.

Next are **guiding roles**—the people who can move ideas into implementation. They can navigate the processes, politics, and other assorted red tape that can hamstring quality ideas. A person with a ninja-like sense for bypassing the pitfalls of organizational ossification is a prime example of a guiding role. Every team, if it wishes to move its ideas into products, needs to develop its guiding skill sets. The person who knows somebody in every department is such a guide. As we discussed with Larry Miller of Activate Networks in the previous chapter, they are assets to the organization. As well, guides are often proselytizers, championing and recruiting others to their projects, as happens in flat organizations like Yammer. Even a great idea needs its defenders. As we noted in the last chapter, the Whitestrips needed a guide through P&G in order to come to market.

Then come the **building roles**—these are the frontline people implementing the strategies developed by people with idea roles. This could be the person laying down lines of code or laying down bricks, writing articles, or interacting with customers. Taken visually, the builders are at the edges of the project, either touching the processes they're building or the relationships with customers.

The **improver role** is the expert of trial and error. When startups talk about "iteration," they're talking about trying new features and rapidly improving upon them. Experiments are especially useful for taking companies into new, possibly nonlinear trajectories, executing on the idea role's suggestions of possible paths. There are many examples. Red Bull's decision to sponsor a man leaping from space to the Earth was a grand experiment. As a reward for its audacity, it dominated media. But not all great ideas need to be so ostentatious. You can don your improver cap to look critically at any aspect of your organization.

How Roles Meet Clusters

Roles and clusters are alike in that they each are temporal, fitting the form of the task at hand, using no more structure than is needed to get the job done. How would each set of personas take part in the visioning, ecological, and implementation clusters? Let's explore that here.

The visioning cluster is the group responsible for sketching out the specifications of a process or product. Such a group needs to have a diversity of skill sets within it to have the whole picture of the potential. Recall how you and your friends went into that darkened room and found different parts of the elephant. Here, idea roles are crucial for their ability to gather all the relevant and potentially disparate knowledge together to inform the development discussion. But scholarly knowledge is not enough for visioning. You also need to know how to get this process through the various layers of the organization, which is where the guiding roles come in. Finally, every product or process has to relate to everything else that the organization has done, which is where the contextualizing of the guides is so necessary.

We need to attach quantifiable metrics to the work of the visioning cluster and the roles within it. Potential metrics could be tracking how many ideas are created within a given time, how many then advance into a state of maturity, and finally, how many are brought to market. We could track the kinds of features we could add to increase users. These metrics lend quantitative rigor to the work of a given team and allow for leaders to track the maturation of a given project. The decisions regarding which metrics should be used for the cluster should be made at the outset of the project—with, of course, everyone's opinion equally weighted.

Next are the heavily networked nodes of the ecological cluster. These are the parts of the organization that are most thoroughly interwoven with the broader ecosystem, and so unique challenges are presented. When executed well, the interconnected nature of the ecological cluster can have powerful effects. If you may recall, the NFL Super Bowl of 2013 suffered a blackout halfway through the championship game. The networks didn't know what to do. But Oreo did. Its "you can still dunk in the dark" tweet was retweeted 15,000 times—showing rapid, real-time marketing aplomb. The cookie had just celebrated its 100th birthday, and so manufacturers had a command center with all of Oreo's agencies assembled for the big game. It was a cluster of narrative-seeing people working in guiding roles. That way, they could respond in real time to the unpredicted events surrounding the game. When the blackout occurred, Oreo literally "saw" it as a chance to "dunk in the dark."[7]

As that example suggests, one of the most immediate roles of the ecological cluster is to increase the presence of an organization's brand. This is readily quantifiable. The metrics we can use could be tracking the size of the audience, the conversion of clicks to interactions to buys, and the movement of retweets and shares.

That leaves us with the implementation cluster, those tasked with bringing the aforementioned vision to its fruition. While ideation role skill sets obviously need to be involved in order to inform the discussion, the majority of the action here will be carried out by the building roles. If we revisit the origin of Crest Whitestrips, we can see there were team members involved that championed and then piloted the new idea through the labyrinths of P&G—a masterful example of system-navigating guidance. When we're faced with such red tape in our working lives, we need to seek the institutional knowledge that will help guide us through bureaucracy and have the interpersonal skills to build consensus along the way. As well, the branding coup of changing Crest from a dental care to an oral care brand shows the narrative expertise of guiding roles.

But, of course, implementation doesn't end there. There's the selling of a given product. This is one of the most readily quantifiable fields. While the ecological cluster's branding efforts created interest, that interest doesn't imply conversion to sales. With the implementation cluster, you're tracking buys and other critical actions. The success threshold will depend on the organization, but you must agree on that before the cluster begins its work. As you continue, you can count the number of leads converted into sales and other metrics.

HOW: BONDS

How should we move within those clusters, like those actors? With velocity. Velocity—the ability to make and implement decisions rapidly—is one of the keys to iteration and innovation. Velocity has many inputs, one of which is the bandwidth provided by quality relationships. In this way, fostering relationships fosters innovation.

Concerning Collaboration

Anyone who has felt dejected after an overdose of ill-run brainstorms wouldn't be surprised to learn that collaboration earned a very bad name during the World Wars—though the extent to which it was initially besmirched is shocking. Taken from the French *collaboration* (itself stemming from the Latin *collaborare*, joining the prefix for "together" and the root for "work"), the word first entered the English vernacular in 1860. During World War II, the word earned a severely negative connotation. A collaborator was someone who worked with occupying Axis forces, especially in France.

But collaboration has happened long before the 19th century. There's a wonderful quote attributed to Charles Darwin: "In the long history of humankind (and animal kind, too) those who learned to collaborate and improvise most effectively have prevailed."[8] And while the aphorism has had its detractors, the history of evolution and of human progress is largely that of lesser and lesser violence and greater and greater collaboration.

As well, collaboration has become an increasing part of the way that businesses operate. While there was once an adversarial relationship between the organization and the "consumer" it was trying to hoodwink, our present era of relentlessly shared information has forced (at least consumer-facing) companies to be as transparent and customer-centric as possible.

But let's focus in on collaboration in the workplace. As with any informed discussion, we will need to define our terms. Let's take our definition from organizational psychologist Leigh Thompson. She writes:

> "True collaboration often calls for periods of focused, independent work interspersed with periods of intense, structured team interaction."[9]

This, we think, is the most satisfying description of the collaborative process. There is a rhythm to collaboration. In the same way that music becomes meaningless if you never hear silence, conversation becomes meaningless if you never have the ability to withdraw into yourself. Similarly, if you dive into an interesting book but never write to or speak to someone about it, you impoverish your understanding of the subject at hand.

When done well, collaboration captures the experience of these two fundamental forms of work. There is a certain "diving deep" feeling to work that we immerse ourselves in when we work in solitude. This is known to anyone from writers to accountants to scientists who enjoy finding themselves immersed in the timelessness of an empty office in the mid-evening. It's that feeling of being able to completely pay the transaction cost of loading the complexity that you are working on into your mind and being able to improvise in solo.

There is something profoundly old about this kind of working alone. Joseph Campbell, the mythologist we discussed earlier, describes the hero's journey as a process of separation from the collective, then a finding or collecting of an item (whether physical or theoretical), and then making a return to society. This is a process at the center of our wisdom traditions. Jesus went to the garden of Gethsemane alone. Siddhartha Gautama went alone to the Bodhi tree to complete his search for truth. And as these religious leaders exemplify, insight is often harvested from insight into the richness of one's internal life. But the journey is not complete if you remain in the wilderness. Whether that knowledge is found within yourself while you are behind the wheel of your car or atop a mountain, you need to bring it back to the people.

Coming back to the people often represents some of the most beautiful images in man and nature: the orchestra moving as a single, swift organism, the basketball team as a constellation of athletes, the colony of ants developing an emergent intelligence together that they never would have touched alone. This, we think, is the hallmark of a highly functioning team. As the saying goes, the whole is greater than the sum of its parts, and the quality created is greater than the quantity assembled. How is this made manifest in an office setting? The craft of journalism may provide us some insight. In *The Art of the Interview*, veteran radioman Martin Perlich talks about how the finest interviews are ones in which a "current of truth" moves between the interviewer and the interviewee.[10] But this need not be left to the whim of conversational mood. As we'll outline in the next chapter, there are ways to structure your face-to-face sessions for maximum potency.

But before we get there, let's take a deep look at the way we interact.

Love Your Colleague?

Barbara Fredrickson is the amiable principal investigator at the University of North Carolina's Positive Emotions and Psychophysiology Lab. She has made it her life's work to understand what's happening inside us when we experience things such as joy and love. Her sunny findings help shine light into the nature of the creative workplace.

What's the place for joy and love in the workplace? The key, again, is to understand what we're optimizing for. If we are seeking innovation, what we want are as many priming factors as possible. We need to relax our inborn and unseen mental rigidity and expand our perspective of a situation beyond the cocoon of "my view" into something more aerial, more aware of the group as a whole (including that of the customer or user, the unseen partner to any workplace conversation).

At the center of Fredrickson's research is what she calls broaden and build theory,[11] which explains the evolutionary adaptive value of positive emotions. What she set out to uncover was the mysterious place positive emotions have in our evolutionary history. While it's obvious that fear leads to the urge to run away and anger leads to the urge to attack, what does an experience like love suggest, especially in a work environment?

While positive emotions don't give the immediate survival feedback of making you run for your life (and living another day), they are a long-term, adaptive investment. According to Fredrickson's research, love, joy, and empathy allow people to have a wider inventory of possible actions. They have a greater ability to take in the broad contexts necessary for systems thinking and help promote psychological resilience.

A peer of Fredrickson's, Cornell researcher Alice Isen has spent two decades researching the effects of positive experiences. One experiment of hers is especially useful for illustrating the way positivity primes for innovative thinking. During the experiment, she tested the clinical reasoning in physicians. Two groups were asked to solve a case of liver disease. One group received a bag of candy to cheer them up. As Fredrickson describes, the physicians who were delighted by the candy were less likely to fixate on their initial ideas about the case, less likely to make a hasty diagnosis, and they absorbed the case information faster. The positive feelings primed more creative, less rigid thinking.[12]

As well, and crucially to our conversation in the business space, positive emotions build what a psychologist would call "social resources," and a layperson would call connections. In the previous chapter, we talked about Activate Networks and their research into the power of relationships, the way that the quantity and quality of a person's network predicts the success of their team. Shared positive emotions are a way to increase the bandwidth of those connections. We all experience this anecdotally. You'll be more apt to entrust responsibilities to the colleagues with whom you feel a closer bond. As well, should the business fail or you lose your job, it's these close connections, these partnerships, that you'll rely on as you move into your next phase.

What's fascinating is that, as Fredrickson and other researchers have described, emotions are not simply something that happens in cognition (aka strictly a feeling) but a mind and body event. Emotional states create changes in the mind and the body, with growing medical evidence of changes in oxytocin and progesterone, two hormones associated with positive feelings. As well, the research of Uri Hasson, a Princeton psychologist, is giving light to the multi-level mirroring that happens between people when they are getting along. Their bodies mirror each other, and their brain activity does as well. Fredrickson calls these moments of mirroring positivity resonance—and it is these micro-moments that she refers to as instances of love—a single event happening in two brains—which she discusses at length in her book *Love 2.0*.

What does that have to do with the way we work? Plenty.

"Creating these micro-moments of positivity resonance with your work colleagues unlocks the collective capacity of the team or the organization by helping everybody expand their mindset," she said in an interview with us. "Develop their skills for learning, co-learning with one another, and as a side benefit to that perspective, to enjoy work more and become healthier in the process."[13]

Armed with this knowledge, how does this affect the way we work? The key is to seek out and be receptive to potential instances for making connections. One of the insights Fredrickson makes is that you can have such a micro moment of love with anyone, whether it's a stranger on the subway, a family member, or yes, your coworker. It's a matter of showing kindness and showing connection. After experiencing these micro-moments, we have a desire to invest in one another's welfare.

We can train ourselves in the ability to make such connections. One of Fredrickson's most notable experiments asked its subjects to record the positive connections they experienced throughout the day. Reporting back later, they had increased feelings of positivity. Over time, this showed an upward spiral. The more often people noted their positive emotions, the more likely they were to experience them. We can infer that making a note of positive experiences is a way to prime future experiences—which, in turn, prime more future positive experiences, which then increases psychological resilience and builds social bonds. This is a great argument for narrating one's workplace experiences, something we'll talk about in depth in the next chapter.

Again, mindfulness plays a tremendous role. You cannot hope to make these moments of connection if you're not there to connect. Whether or not you're texting as you talk to someone, being distracted, or waiting for your turn to talk rather than receiving what the other person is saying, this all undermines the potential for connection. This is a place for what Thich Nhat Hanh called deep listening. Just as a mindfulness meditation is an exercise in observing your thoughts and how you react to them, deep listening is a practice of observing a person's speech and mannerisms and the way you react to them. When we listen deeply to the other person, we can hear them authentically. That authentic connection is the foundation of partnerships.

TAKEAWAYS

People need freedom. To do their best work, people need to feel like they're able to bring all of their effort into the task, which requires an open, autonomy-oriented culture.

People need structure. But this is not anarchy; with freedom comes responsibility. Responsibility can be ensured with both quantitative and qualitative methods, and it springs from a thriving culture.

When people work together, they need togetherness. The pace of progress in an organization depends on the trust among its members. A high-velocity organization will have a culture of shared confidences.

CHAPTER 7

LEADING, SUSTAINING, AND OTHER WAYS TO GROW

"True compassion does not come from wanting to help out those less fortunate than ourselves but from realizing our kinship with all beings."
—Pema Chödrön[1]

A FEW SUMMERS AGO, in the foothills of the Himalayas, a Dutchman named Richard was teaching meditation at Tushita, a retreat center near McLeod-Ganj, the hill-station-turned-tourist-trap that has been the capital of Tibet-in-exile since 1960. Weeks later, the Dalai Lama himself would be giving instructions in his home temple, a twenty-minute walk down the mountain. But for now, we are on a ten-day retreat. The room is a broad, open space, equally temple and classroom. A grand golden Buddha sits behind Richard while rows of a hundred or so assembled students sit before him. He'd be the first to tell you that they're not listening to him; they're listening to 2,500 years of research into mental life.

In the vernacular of the Midwestern United States, Richard would be described as a beanpole, a young man of exceptional height and thinness. He wears his long, light brown hair tied back in a bun. He is given to T-shirts and open collars, flip-flops and kindly laughter. He says that he was once scared of everything. The students can't believe him—being that he just completed a long retreat in the mountains of the Everest region of Nepal. He laughed, and explained that all the tensions in his body released, and his looseness seemed some proof of that.

Today, as usual, Richard is talking about the nature of the mind. The temple is full of students, men and women in their twenties, thirties, forties, and fifties from elsewhere in India, Israel, Europe, East Asia, Australia, and North America. The room still feels spacious despite all the attendants. The walls are the soft canary yellow that Tibetan Buddhists love. Motes of dust spiral in the early afternoon sunlight. The room's stillness is tight with the rapt attention of the students. It's the kind of tranquility you come to India hoping to find.

Then: *whoop!* Richard hops from his cushion like he has just been hit with a water balloon. "There's a sentient being there!" he says, miming the reaction of someone realizing that there's an entire person sitting next to them. The class, you see, is learning about compassion. As we quoted Pema Chödrön earlier, compassion is not a sorrowful, pitying feeling, but realizing the kinship that you have with beings—like the person sitting next to you in this almost silent meditation retreat. They, like you, are experiencing life. They, like you, are alternately proud and worried, anxious and courageous. And when you meditate, especially when sitting in rows together, you can begin to feel that the others are experiencing things just as you are. For non-meditators, similar realizations can be found in your nearest airplane cabin or train car, or, as we like to discuss, in your nearest office. Unless you are in total isolation, wherever you go, sentient beings are there. And sentient beings experience things as you do.

This is key: leadership implies that someone is being led. In the context of an organization, these are people, beings of great sentience, who are participating. To truly lead is to relate to and respect that sentience. Every individual within an organization is a person with consciousness and memory. They have favorite colors, foods, childhood smells, first loves and heartbreaks, parents and grandparents, ambitions and fears, and known and unknown capabilities. If an organization wishes to have the greatest contributions from its individuals, it must not only respect their individuality but appreciate their sentience. For interwoven sentience is the path of innovation, creativity, and sustainability for the organization, as we have argued through this book and will further detail in the following pages.

In the fifth chapter, we introduced the notion of the cluster. It's our answer to the problems of ossification that plague small and large companies trying to cope with the flowing, paradigm-unraveling nature of our present working life. If the world you live in is fluid, you'd better be, too. But only when that fluidity is harnessed with rigor will your outcomes be what you're looking for. In the sixth chapter, we began to fill in that organizational structure with details for how to free the individual worker from creativity-stifling systems and work together in a way that encourages personal and commercial growth. In this, our seventh chapter and the last of this section, we will dig deeper into how people work when they're doing their best work and how leaders can arrange for that culture of flourishing. At the center of this process is appreciating the sentience of the beings you are working with.

What does it mean to lead sentient beings? First, it entails fully appreciating the interior complexity of the people you work with. Then, by appreciating that complexity, you can make explicit the links between a person's individual motivations and that of the organization, creating an alignment and alliance between the individuals that comprise the organization. What we're doing is linking the individual (personal goals like career trajectories) to the collective (group goals like innovation, revenue growth, and impacting the world). To do this, we will need to understand what people need from their work in order to do their best work and how leaders can help arrange that for them. These, then, will be the three movements of this chapter.

So, let's get moving.

WHAT IS IT TO WANT TO WORK VERSUS HAVING TO WORK?

This distinction is rooted in intrinsic versus extrinsic motivation. If you are intrinsically motivated, there is something inside of you that pushes you to work. If you are extrinsically motivated, something outside of you brings you there. (Most people, of course, are both.) The inborn needs for mastery, autonomy, and purpose—these are the sorts of things Dan Pink details in his 2011 hit *Drive*.[2] But that work, of course, is not an exhaustive account of intrinsic factors. We'll build on his and others' insights to understand how to organize around people's growth. Extrinsic motivations, as we know, are often what's being suggested when managers talk about incentivizing a task (money, promotions, and other dangling carrots). As we'll get to later, these intrinsic and extrinsic motivations are more alike than we may assume.

When the mixture of motivating factors is right, miraculous things can happen. An organization can become like a garden in aggressive bloom, where people can thrive and do the best work of their lives.

One of the best expressions of this is the memo that Apple gives new hires, in which the company contrasts work and life's work. "People don't come here to play it safe," the memo printed in the *New York Times* reads. "They come here to swim in the deep end. They want their work to add up to something . . . that couldn't happen anywhere else."[3]

There's something intoxicating about Apple's confidence. We think that organizations should have a similar stride to their step in their own field, to be exemplars of doing the absolute best work. This is what the top performers are attracted to: fully exerting their talents in an environment that encourages and cultivates that skillful exertion (i.e., the Star model described in the first chapter).

We think this is what Evernote CEO Phil Libin means when he talks about how his company doesn't engage in any projects unless they are "sufficiently epic," the kind of projects you'll dedicate yourself to and organize your life around. When pressed for where that terminology comes from, he laughs and talks of growing up with the works of *Lord of the Rings* author J. R. R. Tolkien. Indeed, when organizations are in their highest-functioning state, they are a fellowship of adventurers.

This is at the center of doing work as an extension of your individual emotional convictions, as an expression of your interior life, as spiritual life by way of commerce. This is also the emotional center of the organization, its culture. The culture is made manifest in everything that it creates, in the continually considered excellence of the Mayo Clinic, the multivalent innovation of P&G, and yes, the eminent coolness of Apple. An organization, as we've noted before, is a shared endeavor. One we can build mindfully.

Building Toward Innovation

Naturally, the most immediate way to form an innovative culture is through the people you hire. Since an organization cannot exist without the people in it, and a culture cannot exist without people producing it, it's obvious that people are at the center of an organization's culture. Especially those first few hires. Their demeanor will radiate out into the organization, becoming the default set of actions for new employees.

GitHub, the social coding company, takes this to the extreme. CEO Tom Preston-Werner says that he spends most of his time with hiring, which is done by their sense of taste. They suss out whether candidates share their same aesthetics, valuing autonomy or self-direction, improving as a person, in products, and supporting users. Because of that uniting sense of alignment, GitHub then became a group of self-directed teams, doing work their leadership would have never come up with.[4] With this keen attention to taste, Preston-Werner exhibits an understanding of the way employees experience his organization.

Just as user experience—the way people interact with a product—is becoming increasingly important in the development cycle, employers need to become more mindful of the way employees experience the organization. This, you could say, is a primary way to acknowledge the sentience of the individuals that compose it. To do that, we need to consider what people are looking for in an employer and in their working experience.

Yes, a paycheck is an obvious motivator. But it is not the ultimate one. A growing body of research shows how the correlation between monetary wealth and self-reported happiness drops off over time. A 2010 study, led by economist Angus Deaton and psychologist Daniel Kahneman, made headlines with its finding that a salary of $75,000 was the threshold for day-to-day happiness. They concluded that at that income threshold, people could better absorb adversities as diverse as asthma or divorce, thus predicting happiness.[5] As well, a 2012 poll by the Marist Institute for Public Opinion found that respondents with an income level over $50,000 reported higher levels of satisfaction with their safety, health, employment, community involvement, and spiritual life—suggesting that that is the threshold.[6]

To put it into technical philosophical terms, being paid well is probably a necessary part of being happy and fully engaged—it certainly provides a strong signal—but it is not sufficient to ensure that state. There's more going on to engagement than just compensation. So, what else are people looking for in their jobs, how do we give it to them, and how does this relate to doing amazing, innovative work? Let us explore.

Where the Individual Meets the Organization

As we've contended before, part of leadership is having an organization-wide mindfulness. This is not only in the way that customers, users, and patrons experience the organization but also in the ways in which team members do. What presence does the organization have in their lives? How do they relate to it? How do the ideas and narratives they hold about themselves relate to those of the organization? Part of this is alignment—the taste that GitHub vigilantly seeks—and another is the time people are spending with our organizations. Specifically, we need to be transparent about the way organizations and individuals link themselves together.

The idea of the company man is now resting peacefully in the dustbin of history. Though we value commitment, the organization is no longer a parental, redeemer figure that will nurture an employee for a lifetime. The innovation economy is also, it seems, the gig economy. People are working for shorter and shorter periods with given organizations. What we need is greater transparency about this situation.

Reid Hoffman (of LinkedIn fame) and his collaborators Ben Casnocha and Chris Yeh have proposed such an idea: a new contract between employers and employees that they like to call "tours of duty." Acknowledging the impermanent nature of an employer/employee relationship, they still want to promote trust and investment between the individual and the collective. Rather than sharing loyalty, both sides have an alliance.

"As allies, employer and employee try to add value to each other," they wrote in *Harvard Business Review*. "The employer says, 'If you make us more valuable, we'll make you more valuable.' The employee says, 'If you help me grow and flourish, I'll help the company grow and flourish.'"[7]

There is an honesty and Hammurabi-like clarity to the arrangement. I help you guys get better, and you guys help us get better. It's an honoring of the temporality of working together and of life, a de-romanticizing and de-fixation of organization as savior. Instead, we have an arrangement more truly in alignment with the way things are today.

Since an organization is made of people—not the name of the brand or the building it stands in—it stands to reason that when the people grow, the organization grows. Over the past few chapters, we have discussed the ways in which people grow in their personal and professional lives. As leaders, we're trying to arrange our organizations in ways that create a mutual flourishing between their different parts.

This, we think, is what the word "engagement" is beginning to scratch the surface of. When people are doing the work that expands their skill sets and sense of self and that they feel is meaningful to the world, then they will be deeply invested in the work they do. This is the difference between having to work and getting to work, between having a job and developing a vocation. We want everyone in our fellowship to be practicing their vocations.

Adjacent to this is recognizing that every professional is engaged in managing their own career. Every person is yearning for advancement. The savvy leader, then, is the one who recognizes how to help their employees advance themselves by way of the organization. Nihal Mehta, the former CEO of LocalResponse, is one.

Mehta is a serial entrepreneur, and like many serial entrepreneurs, the readiest description for him is "ball of energy." He's handsome, quick to laugh, and whip-smart. LocalResponse, a targeted advertising startup, is his fifth company. He says that after a while, you get better at running these things. Over the years, the role of the CEO has become apparent to him.

"My No. 1 job is to make sure everyone is operating at their absolute potential," he says on a sunny October day in New York.[8] Mehta says that his job is to make sure everyone is "incredibly passionate" about what they do. Everything else falls into place after that.

In noting this, Mehta models one part of what leaders in the innovation economy need to do. If we are trying to organize teams of people who will give their fullest effort—and not in a punishment-oriented, extrinsic reward system, but in a fulfillment-oriented, intrinsically motivated context—we need to find people who will throw themselves into their work and then find how the organization can fit into their lives.

"I assume you're a rock star engineer because you've gotten this far," Mehta says. "But are you super passionate, is this your life mission to do what you're doing?"

From Mehta's fervor, it's clear he is.

"And also, can I give you a growth path into something you would like to be in two or three years?" he continues. "Would you like to run the tech team? Would you like to come up with new patents? Would you like to create new algorithms?"

Mehta wants people that have, like him, found their niche in the universe. In this way, much of the job of the leader is to become a curator of talent, to find the talented people who can do their best work in the environment of your organization. Curation has, in our hypertextual world, had a change in meaning. When bloggers aggregate and repurpose existing material, they are curating it. (Maria Popova of Brain Pickings, Annie Murphy Paul of the Brilliant Report, and Jason Hirschhorn of Media ReDEFined are all examples of some of the best in the young craft.) But, of course, the term has much older roots. From the 14th century, the medieval Latin is *curate*, a person responsible for the care of souls; or *curator*, an overseer, manager, or guardian. It was originally the person in charge of minors or lunatics. Finally, in the 16th century, it took on the meaning of an "officer in charge of a museum, library, etc.," which is the definition mostly met before the advent of hypertext and the electronic interlinking that followed.

If you walk into an art gallery, from the Museum of Modern Art to a local show, you will find yourself (at least, we hope) in a curated space such that the overall effect of the works in the room will be greater than the sum of its parts. There will be, in other words, a synergy among the exhibition's components and their arrangement. An additional value will be added by the way the pieces are put together.

The work of the leader parallels that of the ancient maritime navigator, moving from port to port by drawing the constellations in the sky. We should look for new ways to combine and recombine the talents available within an organization. One of these ways is the clustering discussed in the previous two chapters. We can find out which people work well together by placing them or allowing them to opt into new working situations. Perhaps they will even surprise themselves.

As well, if we are in a larger organization, we can (as curators) exercise the power of combinatorial creativity by arranging talent from different sectors within an organization, and thus relating ideas and potentially entire disciplines that would have been previously distinct from one another—just as P&G did with its Crest Whitestrips. They also need to find how an individual's trajectory converges with that of the organization, as Mehta encouraged. Leaders need to always be looking for where the next product line may be lying latent and ready to be discovered—catalyzed by their efforts of curation.

The Arts and Arcs of Trajectory

Trajectory

Putting together a team that works at its absolute potential is more than arranging individual talent in novel ways. We must also recognize the drive of the people involved. Engagement is also velocity. If someone is fully immersed in what they are doing, they will work with the greatest force and speed they can. But it is frivolous to think that the worker is spending their scarce time in order to create value for the organization and make their managers look good. Rather, they are trying to achieve something for themselves, somewhere along the hierarchy of needs. The most immediate of these is that of the career arc.

This is where Hoffman, Casnocha, and Yeh meet with Mehta: this acknowledgment that what an organization provides a worker is the opportunity to grow. But, as any parent will understand, with growth comes departure. A teenager graduates from high school; a young adult graduates from college; an adult graduates (with less official ceremony) from position to position, stage to stage, within a career. This is perhaps understood within the way we talk about career development. Setting off on their own, the entrepreneur is an alumna of PayPal; the independent consultant, having built their reputation at BCG, becomes an alumnus when they decide to go freelance. Every major shift is a graduation.

The task for a leader is to be direct and open with workers regarding every person's trajectory in the organization. Is there a space possibly opening? Would an implementation-person make a fine manager, and have they demonstrated leadership qualities, rather than simply a prowess at their craft? Or, for the entrepreneurial worker, can they create a greater role from within the organization? Or could they launch their own venture and take on the larger organization as a first client? How do these individual and collective futures fit together?

Some kind of unexamined sense of propriety made these conversations taboo within the workplace. Just as it is thought impolite to acknowledge that one's life will be over some day in the future, it's impolite to acknowledge that one's role within an organization—and the organization itself—will one day be gone. One of the duties of the humanistic leader, then, is to open up this initially uncomfortable conversation, to acknowledge the way trajectories join and part. The other side of trajectory is to show how the progress of the individual links to the progress of the whole.

THE TWO LAYERS OF PROGRESS

Sometimes the greatest of insights for one field come from another. Such is the case of ingesting *How to Read a Book*, the genteel, thoughtful, and thorough guide to critical reading by Mortimer J. Adler and Charles Van Doren, originally published in 1940. The work is an indispensable guide to reading for learning, understanding, and wisdom. But one passage partway through is arresting in its simplicity and for how it relates to working together.[9]

For Adler and Van Doren, books are indispensable because they are absent teachers. For those of us no longer in school, we must often rely on the written word in order to accelerate our understanding of life. To that end, the authors argue that the teacher's profession is parallel to two other noble ones: that of the farmer and the physician.

The farmer is in the business of growing plants, the physician of curing patients, the teacher in educating students. But the very grammar of those clauses betrays a misunderstanding. The farmer does not grow the plant; the plant does. The physician does not make the patient healthier; the patient grows healthier. And the teacher cannot command the pupil to learn; that growth must happen within the student.

Instead, what these noble professions do is arrange the circumstances for the beings they are caretaking—or curating, if we can use the word in its older Latin meaning—so that they may flourish. Put pithily, you cannot tell a flower to grow, but you can help it to. The farmer is mindful of the seasons and plants seeds when most suited. The physician understands a patient's case history and integrates treatment within that larger context. The teacher understands where the student is coming from and can make the material relatable.

The manager can be added to that list. The people we work with are not so unlike the plants the farmer grows, the pupils the teacher teaches, or the patients the doctor treats. To stretch the agricultural metaphor, you cannot tell any of the flowers, cucumbers, or corn stalks in your office to grow. The growing happens within them. And one does not need to be a leader or manager in title to encourage the growth of others. We simply need to be people of action.

So, how do we lead and manage in ways that help people grow rather than tell people to grow? To want to work, rather than have to work? By looking at the forefront of organizational theory, we can see that it's actually a matter of managing progress, not people.

PRINCIPLES OF PROGRESS

Teresa Amabile is a professor and a director of research at Harvard Business School. For decades, her work focused on the nature of creativity, though as of late, her focus has shifted to the inner lives of people at work. She studies how we relate to our achievements, both as individuals and within organizations. She has published in both the academic and popular press, perhaps most notably with *The Progress Principle*, coauthored with her husband, Steven Kramer.

Her research—including one study of 238 individuals making nearly 12,000 diary entries—skewers the widely held idea that fear and high pressure ensure achievement. Instead, as she writes in one essay for *Harvard Business Review*, knowledge workers are more creative when they have a positive experience of work, when they think well of their organization and colleagues, and when they find their work to be meaningful—and thus intrinsically motivating. And when they are achieving, when they are making progress.[10]

It doesn't need to be monumental. While there are indeed heroic moments within a career, Amabile notes that a more commonplace victory can be enough—for example, a programmer rooting out a difficult bug. We can extrapolate this to other cases: the nonprofit director making a draft of a grant application, the high school teacher finishing a day without having to raise their voice, the executive wrapping up their tasks in time to have dinner with their family. When people have these slow, steady, and daily markers of progress, they feel fulfilled, and they end the day looking forward to the next one, rather than walking out of the office door with an undead shuffle.

Just as the farmer tills the soil in order to help seeds germinate, the manager can help arrange the workflow of their direct reports to help meaningful progress take root.

Meaningful Tillage

Meaningful progress can happen in a number of ways.

Our first suggestion is to incorporate opportunities for narrated work—as in creating mechanisms for people to be able to describe the work they are doing on a daily basis—removing the need for higher-ups to check in on their progress. One of the best examples is a startup called iDoneThis, which sends an email at the end of the day simply asking what you accomplished that day. That little ritual creates intrinsic motivation, CEO Walter Chen tells us.[11] People can see the small movements toward growth every day, and their teams can see what they did and when.

Another crucial element is the time-bound nature of clusters. As we have laid out over the past two chapters, clusters are teams whose life is tied to the task they are completing. Since the cluster only lasts for so long, they conclude with the group breaking up. This is an event that marks the growth of the people involved, who can then bask in the glory of a job well done and reflect on what did or didn't go right.

Lastly, and perhaps most traditionally, is the notion of having soft contact between leaders and reports. We've spoken about how relationships are the bandwidth by which information transfers. One form of that bandwidth is the normalization of interactions of people across the hierarchy. It should be normal for you to talk to your boss. Ideally, that will make constructive criticism a non-heroic practice, which accelerates the speed at which an organization can improve.

This communality can be built in a number of ways, whether it's an after-work beer or coffee or, perhaps more healthfully, a midday walk taken together. The key is to allow the interactions to become normal enough that it's not a big deal to spend time together. That casualness signals trust between the individuals within a group. This is how you build the fellowship. This is how you go on the sufficiently epic quest.

TAKEAWAYS

Workers are sentient beings. You cannot have an organization without sentient beings inside of it. Deeply linked is the relationship between the appreciation of the sentience of the people you work with and the power of your organization.

Leaders curate talent. Building an organization is the gathering of people for a common cause. When the right people are gathered in the right way, the whole becomes greater—perhaps much greater—than the sum of its parts. Gathering the right people together at the right time is curation.

People need progress. Underlying the awards, honors, and bottom lines is every person's need to feel growth. To lead with precision, then, is to mindfully cultivate that growth. The awards, honors, and bottom lines will follow.

PART THREE

PART THREE

FLOWING IDEAS, GROUNDED DECISIONS, AND LONG-BURNING VALUE

THERE'S AN OLD CHINESE saying that when you've made it ninety percent down the path, you're halfway to your destination. The frustration you feel from the statement's oddly true logic reflects the frustration inherent in completing any major project. The last little bit is always the most difficult. The last few steps are where our faith may falter, and we may lose what we set out to do in the first place, like Orpheus of Greek legend losing his love for lack of trust. With a full appreciation of the difficulty of completion, let us set out to complete this act of our odyssey.

In our first section, we sketched out the landscape we now find ourselves in: stormy waters, strong tides, and stronger winds. But that elemental energy can be harnessed if we establish a productive, sustainable, and positive relationship with our own interior working lives and then allow that to extend into the way we interact with the people we work with. Part of that was recognizing how damn long it takes to do anything worthwhile. We need to build our organizations in such a way that they can be sustainably innovative and consistently new.

In our second section, we explored the ins and outs of what such a place might look like—and how you'd act when you got there. We discovered that much of the product you make is predicted by the structure that created it. And we discovered that the traditional doesn't match well to our insistently fluid present. We also realized the ways we interact with one another could predict creativity, innovation, and resilience, and so we sought to act congruently to that understanding. Taking those points together, we carved out what a leader of such an organic, rigorous system might look like and how we can embody that ideal.

Now, we enter into the last phase, where we will be unpacking the doing of work in an unpredictable world with exemplary people. In the eighth chapter lies the mysterious process of ideation—the way in which we can be constantly finding new ideas, ideas that can become strategy. Then, in the ninth chapter, we will use a process we call blueprinting to get explicit about finding the strategies that work. In our tenth chapter, we will uncover the tangible and intangible qualities of creating value over the long term. And we will discover how to incorporate that understanding into our individual and organizational working lives.

It's time to complete the journey.

CHAPTER 8

CREATING CONSTANT CREATION

"In a dark and profound unity."
—Baudelaire[1]

IDEAS ARE THE BEGINNING of strategy. Fascinatingly, the process of their discovery is quite parallel, though not identical, between individuals and organizations. One informs the other. Fundamentally, the continuous discovering, planning, and implementing of ideas is how innovation becomes sustainable.

Just as our first two sections moved between the working life of the individual and that of the organization and tried to show the interlinking between the two, this third section will map the way a concept can mature into its reality, both as individuals and as groups. This, we hope, will empower the way you work within yourself and the work you do within a team.

When your authors were first discussing which individual to frame this idea-to-reality process around, there were naturally thoughts of contemporary entrepreneurs and their well-worn trials and travails: Bezos, Jobs, Zuckerberg, and the like. But after some consideration, we have decided to go with a much more alternative, though perhaps even more central, figure—Leonardo da Vinci. Why?

There are a number of reasons. First, as Nassim Taleb would argue,[2] things that have remained relevant for a long, long time will most likely remain relevant into the future. Consider the way that sandals and kitchenware haven't really changed since the Ancients, or that the fundamental problems of philosophy—the existence of the divine, the meaning of life, the nature of goodness and suffering—remain unresolved. Whereas a Nokia phone, a Palm Pilot, and a Motorola pager are all little more than paperweights now. If we're trying to explore something fundamental about the way that people and organizations create, then it makes sense to study one of the timeless creative figures and yoke that timelessness to deeply timely examples.

With this intention, we enter into the third part of our journey. In the first phase, we described the mindset needed for individuals and organizations to work in a way that is good for intrapersonal, interpersonal, and financial well-being. In the second phase, we traced the infrastructure for carrying that work out, then organized around creativity, innovation, and sustainability. Now, in this third part, we will describe how to bring the ideas generated by these techniques to life in three phases. First, with concepts, the beginning of strategy. Then blueprinting, the carrying out of strategy. And finally, value realization, the continuing of strategy.

In this chapter, we will be taking a deep dive into understanding how to find, capture, and organize concepts. In the same way only a single sperm among many finds an egg, only a single concept from a whole harvest of ideas will one day be born into the market. This is why we need to create volleys of ideas and have many seeds readily available, which can then be funneled into reality. Though, as we'll see in the next chapter, insights may need to be reborn.

RIGOROUS CHAOS, ORDERLY EMERGENCE, AND FLORENCE

We often tend to think of creativity as a reckless, messy process. It's the enemy of order and a rebellion against the structures of life. But, as we've mentioned earlier, you can think of creativity as a volatile process. It is a sort of randomness, an unknowability, that you are welcoming into your experience, the raw vulnerability of the previously unknown soon being made known. Since creativity is a sort of vulnerability and a constructive species of volatility, we must create security around it—and, in this way, nurture it.

When we do this, discipline becomes nourishing. Rigor becomes constructive. As we discussed in chapter three, at an evolutionary, neurophysiological level, we read volatility as danger. This is why, as a sort of unexamined adaptation, people who work in insecure environments—if their jobs, power, or salary are in danger—cannot help not inviting volatility into their experiences. In this way, they prevent themselves from ever being able to improve on what already is, to reach into the unknown, to innovate.

As we have quoted the Zen Master Shunryu Suzuki before, discipline is creating situations. And to extend on the agricultural metaphors of chapter seven, one person cannot force another to grow, to create, or to offer up something new. One can only help provide for the situation for the new to arrive.

The first element of systematizing discovery is to ensure that a system of security is already in place for people to do their work. They must be financially, emotionally, professionally, and spiritually stable so they may then bring in the instability of stretching themselves, their ideas, and their performance—for decades. Having a nuanced understanding of and equally nuanced application of the reciprocal relationship between security and volatility in creative work is one of the necessary conditions for systematizing discovery.

Discovery, again, is an emergent process. While you can be deliberate in the way you arrange for discovery to happen, you cannot command new ideas to emerge since, by definition, it is an entry from the unknown (and thus uncommendable) into the known. But you can court the unknown in the way the bee courts the flower. If you do so well, the unknown will yield its pollen. Let's systematize the courting.

Rooting Out Ideas: Cultivating Curiosity

If an idea is the seed of strategy, then what is the seed of an idea? It is experience. But can there be qualitative differences in experience? There can. Research has shown that the reason time seems to "speed up" as you get older is that the world is not as novel as it was when you were young.[3] The more familiar you are, or you perceive you are with a situation, the quicker you will experience it. This is an argument for varied experience—a predictor of creativity—but it is also an argument for mindfulness.

How? Because it is a matter of attending to your experience. The less we're wrapped up in our thinking, the more we notice about the world. What do you call this attending to experience? Curiosity. As Einstein famously said that he had no special talent beyond being passionately curious, we can say that there is no other avenue to cultivating creative work aside from impassioned curiosity. Thankfully, we have models for this way of living, with Leonardo da Vinci as one of the foremost.

Since we'll be spending a long time with him over these next few pages, let's call the master by his familiar name, Leonardo. Upon getting to know him, something strange will happen. With familiarity, the myth that cloaks this man who has been made immortal will begin to dissipate, and the complex, anxious, beautiful mortal that actually lived will be revealed in some small way. In this way, it's a little bit like falling in love. Knowing another's insecurities and mistakes somehow brings you closer to that person. There's an intimacy in failure. And Leonardo, with his titanic successes, also knew great failure. He regretted on his deathbed not giving enough time to his art. For the main framing of his life, we are indebted to the foundational scholarship of the French writer Serge Bramly, who spent five years writing a 400-page tome called *Leonardo*, a book of grace and depth without which we would not be able to mine the deeply lived wisdom of the Renaissance man's life.[4] For further reading, please see the notes in the back of *Everything Connects*.

Leonardo was born on April 15, 1452. In his lifetime, a new continent would be discovered, and much of modern life would begin to take shape. Dante's *Inferno* would become popular throughout Italy. Later in his life, Leonardo would meet a young courtier named Niccolo Machiavelli, and we can be reasonably sure that some of the artist's ideas made it into *The Prince*. As the word "Renaissance" would suggest, a resurgent interest in the arts and the natural world would take hold, supported by religious, public, and private wealth. And yet this was, in many ways, still the Middle Ages, as calamities like the Black Plague and rather unnecessary warfare were all to be expected. The time was not so unlike our own. Leonardo, in order to make his works, would find "protectors" in the forms of dukes, princes, and a pope (not too different from the way that an entrepreneur seeks funding today, whether from venture capitalists or banks). More deeply, that time saw the same hierarchy of needs that entrepreneurs tend to today. To survive financially, to create wealth, and to make an impact upon the world were just as present in Leonardo's life.

Beginning as a painter, before he became a sculptor, engineer, anatomist, and painter again, he was long trained in experiencing and appreciating the natural world. Thus, the power of his representations. This observational enthusiasm informed all of his work. If you were to peer into his notebooks, you would find the movement of water that fueled his lifelong preoccupation with hydraulics, his foundational studies of the workings of the human body, and even the faces of the people he encountered in Florence, Rome, Milan. As he once wrote:

"I roamed the countryside searching for answers to things I did not understand. Why shells existed on the tops of mountains along with the imprints of coral and plants and seaweed usually found in the sea. Why the thunder lasts a longer time than that which causes it, and why immediately on its creation the lightning becomes visible to the eye while thunder requires time to travel. How the various circles of water form around the spot which has been struck by a stone, and why a bird sustains itself in the air. These questions and other strange phenomena engage my thought throughout my life."

His emphasis on observation was so great that he would reconceive the way we perceived perception. As the page of his notebook shows, he looked closely at the looking itself. His understanding of the way light lands upon the eye pushed against the prevailing theories of optics, those passed down by the Platonic tradition and held by contemporary scholars. While the old way saw the eye as sending a beam of vision into the world, Leonardo saw the eye as something that received light, as illustrated here.

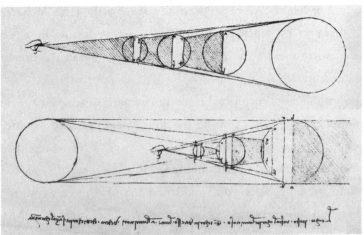

"Light and Shade" by Leonardo Da Vinci.
Image courtesy of Encore Editions, www.encore-editions.com.

That is the power of curiosity and observation. Under examination, even the most respected of received wisdom gives way. Innovation so much springs from having an insight born of close attendance to people's behavior. If we can remember, the Swiffer was born after Continuum (the consultancy Procter & Gamble called in to discover a new home product) studied the way that people cleaned their homes and found that people spent as much time cleaning their mops as they spent cleaning with their mops. So, they moved to solve that pain point. Now, sprucing up your kitchen only takes a matter of minutes, given a good Swiffering. In another domestic example, Febreze took off when marketers realized that people felt proud after finishing their chores. So, they supplied a ritual to conclude them, a satisfying spray that now makes more than $1 billion a year.[5] Persistent inquiry clearly has its payoffs.

Diverse Experience

As Leonardo's observation-filled notebooks evidence, the first phase of taking a concept to its fruition as a value for a user is to invent the concept in the first place. As we have talked about before, most of creativity is combinatorial, as in, new things are found by combining (or finding the relationship) between two unrelated things. Consider again the way that P&G founded its Crest Whitestrips product line. This suggests that the heart of the innovation process is to attend closely to the various events occurring around you and plot the connections formed by them, the same way the ancients mapped the constellations. We're trying to find just how everything connects, and we're ferreting out the latent value residing in those connections.

The creativity-spurring benefits of diverse experiences (and diverse individuals) can be realized at both an individual and organizational level. Let's get into how.

What is it that makes some people more creative than others? A 2013 study in the *Creativity Research Journal* helps shed some light. Researchers

Edward Nęcka and Teresa Hlawacz wanted to test the effects of temperament and divergent thinking on sixty visual artists and sixty bank officers.[6] Temperament, in psychology, is thought to be the part of your personality that is innate rather than learned. Traits lie in introversion or extroversion. Divergent thinking is a process in which you're generating ideas by exploring many solutions, like free-writing or associative thinking. This is unlike convergent thinking, where you're making logical steps to arrive at a conclusion.

What did they find? As Scott Barry Kaufman of *Scientific American* reports,[7] the bank officers were about average when it came to divergent thinking, while the artists were top-notch at creating new pictures and words.

What's more fascinating, though, is that artists were quite similar to the bankers in their temperament, although a few artists had high scores within both divergent thinking and temperament. Those with the highest scores had the following temperament traits.

- **Briskness:** "quick responding to stimuli, high tempo of activity, and the ability to switch between actions."

- **Endurance:** "an ability to behave efficiently and appropriately in spite of intense external stimulation or regardless of the necessity to pay attention during prolonged periods of time."

- **Activity:** "the generalized tendency to initiate numerous activities that lead to, or provoke, rich external stimulation; it is conceived as the basic regulator of the need for stimulation."

For the researchers, the most crucial of these traits was activity. Postulating that temperament is a foundation for the development and expression of a person's creative potential, they found that people with a high activity score often "have many diverse experiences that may be used as a substrate for divergent thinking and creative activity."[8] We're taken with this idea of diversity begetting a substrate.

Taken from biology, the substrate is the base that an organism lives on. Plants have a substrate of the soil. Our experiences, then, are a kind of substrate from which we can draw our connections or base our convergent and divergent thinking, and they are the source from which we can empathize with others. It's what we're talking about when we describe the feeling of "going through something together."

While Leonardo traveled little, he had a breadth of closely attended experiences. His curiosity drove him to observe and discover and, in turn, create. His foundational studies in anatomy (which, late in his life, a rival would accuse him of practicing necromancy for) informed his breathtaking representationalism. If you saunter through a gallery of Renaissance paintings, most of them paint the Christ child as a small adult, lending the viewer's experience an unsavory cognitive dissonance. But Leonardo, in one of his era-defining innovations, did not follow that traditional precedent and instead painted from life, utilizing the game-changing Renaissance technology of perspective.

If you take in *The Last Supper*, you will find that Christ's head is placed precisely at the picture's vanishing point, giving the fresco a profound unity of composition. As well, if you consider the earlier *Annunciation*, as Serge Bramly does, you will notice that while previous depictions of angel's wings appear to be cumbersome "theatrical accessories," Leonardo's grow from shoulder blades, "naturally prolonging the line of the arm." These and other paintings—not to mention his engineering works—evidence a substrate of experience of legendary health.

So, how do we tend ours? Let's consult an expert in living omnivorously.

INTENTIONALLY OMNIVOROUS

Brooklyn: Friday, 8:30 a.m. It's an early summer rain. There are puddles, cobblestones, iPhones. A gaggle of young creatives gathers around a small

hall with a faintly Grecian facade. We're at the edge of the area known as
DUMBO ("Down Under the Manhattan Bridge Overpass"), the geek-
chic neighborhood just across the East River from Manhattan.

After gathering necessary coffees and making awkward attempts at
sitting and talking to each other, the crowd welcomes to the stage an
ethereal, energetic woman: chef-designer-photographer-philosopher-en-
trepreneur Emilie Baltz. With her light hair cut short and swooped to one
side, she looks a bit like a comic book heroine, and as she tells us about
her life—of being raised by a French mother and American father in the
Rust Belt town of Joliet, Illinois—she becomes more and more heroic. She
makes food that reshapes how we think about food. In so doing, she is a
case study for us in the way that the experiences you take in become the
work that you produce.

In the simplest, most profound of ways, her book *Junk Foodie: 51 Delicious Recipes for the Lowbrow Gourmand* is a representation of hybridized
upbringing. The sangria is made with grape soda, Fun Dip, and Kool-Aid;
pralines are made of Reese's Cups and Fruit Roll-ups; and a Napoleon,
the traditional French confection, is made with potato chips and a highly
finessed Twinkie. Her clients have included AOL, eBay, Microsoft, Pana-
sonic, and *Vogue* magazine, to name a few. The work she creates is many
things all at once. And, as she explains in an interview weeks after her
talk, much of that highly differentiated, highly innovative output comes
from having a range of inputs. This, Baltz says, is a mark of omnivory, the
practice of being omnivorous—of "eating all."[9]

Echoing our finding that part of creativity is discipline, Baltz first
started describing her process as an omnivorous one in the fall of 2009.
Searching for a mission statement, she came up with omnivorous. It made
sense, since she grew up eating any and everything.

"It is about balance," she says. "It is about openness, it is about curiosity,
it is about responsiveness, and within all of that, it has to do with flexibility.
So, the fact that one is omnivorous means that one can go to many places

and experience many people at many levels. I don't love to eat a lot of meat, but I can travel through many cultures. The choice of omnivory is a choice to communicate and have a choice with people."

This ties back to a discussion that we've been having throughout this book. People connect with people—and create things for people—when they feel a sense of kinship, of shared experience between one another. Empathy is the most direct understanding. In this way, entrepreneurship, if we are to be creating products and services of value to a range of cohorts, is an omnivorous endeavor. As Baltz describes it, being intentional about the breadth of experiences you give yourself allows you to better understand yourself, which helps clarify the foundation of this process. Whether we're designers, cooks, project managers, or, yes, a writer, sampling a range of experiences helps us to identify ourselves within that context, to find again our place in the world.

"Being able to taste many different ways of writing, all these different mediums, allows you to get out of yourself and see yourself," she says. "Being an eater of everything, it's a form of identity building. If you touch on everything, the dots do start to connect."

Baltz is reminded of her drawing professor back in school, telling her that it's not about the lines that emerge from her pencil but that space in between the lines where the image is made. That absence is presence; that negative space is most ripe with meaning.

With the tasting of all, she says, "it's not the all that defines the end product." Rather, it's that negative space, "in the chunks in between A and B and Z and K, that suddenly you start to take shape, between no one individual, brand, or culture. But by being open to those influences that come and go, they ricochet off of pieces of you, and you see what you are made of."

An ongoing part of identity building—for us in both our individual working lives and as part of a team—is to practice experiencing a breadth of experiences, a pool of experiences from which we can draw on later in life. When journalists ask artists the hack question of "where do your ideas come from?" the answer can only be this: our experiences.

"The natural human existence is not monosyllabic," she says. "We must lead omnivorous lives. Every ecosystem is like that, from micro to macro."

Dating Ideas: Getting Practical about Courting Emergence

As the lives of Baltz, Leonardo, and the Swiffer mop suggest, there are great benefits to be found in closely attending to a varied life and noting your discoveries. It behooves us, then, to start turning that aspirational curiosity into knowledge-discovering action, both as individuals and in groups.

If we take Baltz and her confections as a model, we can make our lives more omnivorous by diversifying its various aspects. Drawing from Baltz's insight, we can arrange for more innovation-generating omnivory in our lives by diversifying the following:

- **The media you consume.** Taking in a range of art, news, and scholarship makes you more vulnerable to cross-pollinating insight. If you normally read about business, take in the arts. If you usually watch self-serious documentaries, grab some popcorn and catch a blockbuster. If you've never seen a ballet, see one. If you don't get the point of botanical gardens, go there and find it.

- **The people you see.** Network theory has found that the success of a team is predicted by the quality and quantity of the connections that members have—especially across disciplines and other silos. To apply that to our personal lives, we'd benefit from growing diverse partnerships within our lives. Yes, a true partner is a rare thing indeed, but that preciousness is part of the reason to vigilantly care for them.

- **The events you attend.** Finding those partnerships—the members of your tribe, if you will—is as difficult as it is life-affirming. The question, then, is where do people in your interest and priority circle congregate? Conferences, talks, and readings are all examples, and so is your friendly neighborhood bar. Same with parties, dinner or otherwise. The idea is that conferences and parties are places where serendipity makes itself available, ready to be realized by a friendly smile and a heartfelt handshake.

But these are only three ways to enrich our lives with broader, more closely attended experiences. We can also become more deliberate about training ourselves in directly participating in our experiences—that is, living a little bit more mindfully. In the United States, at least, yoga has become normalized, and meditation is following that process as well. Beyond helping us gain a greater intimacy with our minds, pursuing such practices in a group setting avails us to another asset—the companionship of finding fellow travelers along the path.

BREADTH, DEPTH, AND ORGANIZATIONS

Just as Leonardo came to make realizations about his world by attending closely to it, we can make realizations about our organizations by attending closely to them. We can look for the realities sitting adjacent to what presently is and, in this way, root out possibilities. But this is not done by sitting alone in your room and pondering, though that's certainly part of the process.

In the same way Leonardo would wander about the squares of Italy inquiring of what was there, so too can we make inquiries of the places, people, and processes with which we work. This kind of organizational mindfulness is born of implicit and explicit knowledge sharing, the kinds encouraged by the clustering tactics we discussed in part two. But no matter the degree of habitual functionality you have, it can be productive to make a direct inquiry into these aspects of an entrepreneur's reality.

As we've discussed before, innovation springs from and is shepherded by people. In chapter seven, we described the potential value promised by unshackling people from their job prescriptions—that by removing the boundary boxes of what a person is capable of, they will naturally be free to do more (so long as there is proper alignment to a shared goal, as agreed upon by the group). What this leads to is a democratization of idea generation. While not everyone is going to be a part of the visioning cluster, everyone should be thinking about the vision of the organization and their place within it, and everyone will be doing so if the proper architecture is assembled.

The systemization of creativity is actually a democratization. Recall how Yammer's ephemeral organization structure, by virtue of its rotationality, detaches people from their one job and exposes them to other roles, both in implementation and in leadership. Adam Pisoni told us that the rotational structure "gets everybody thinking about the system." That sort of organizational awareness—and the experimentation that can follow—frees people from assuming that the role prescriptions they're working in fell from the sky, that it's "just the way it is." In this way, that unending curiosity that gave Leonardo a need to tinker can be opened up within each person in an organization, with a permission to create radiating out from leadership.

But before you can structure an organization, we need an organization—that is, people. Continuous idea generation is again an aspect of being a curator of talent. We need to find and welcome wide-ranging minds and give them the freedom and the motivation to range about, as Nihal Mehta and Teresa Amabile might say. You cannot tell a flower to grow—let alone to have an appetite for knowledge like a Renaissance master—but you can find those passionately curious people. And it is with these fine individuals that we make partnerships and alliances with, as the

Medicis, Ludovico Sforza, and Cesare Borgia did with Leonardo. When we are lucky enough to find talent—in ourselves and in others—we nourish it.

Keep Recording

If you're lucky enough to visit the Metropolitan Museum of Art on Manhattan's Upper East Side, it would be unconscionable to not wander into the easterly part of the museum, where the most staggering message from the past stands freely in an open atrium: The Temple of Dendur. Dating from 15 BCE, it spans eighty-two feet in length and is decorated with lotus flowers and images of Isis, Osiris, and other deities. The temple is powerfully preserved—you can't help but be taken aback by it. Fascinatingly, the "king" at the time was Caesar Augustus of Rome, who naturally had himself depicted as a pharaoh. This is a house handed down from millennia—an artifact.

As the rest of the museum attests, all we really have left from former times are their artifacts, or, as the Latin suggests, "the things that were made." When we say that talk is cheap, we really mean that talk disappears. The artifacts stay with us. While something about the bubbling bursts of creativity are short-lived in nature, professional creativity finds ways to be lasting. What we need is to be constantly generating artifacts of the concepts we come up with—or, as Google Ventures says, to "always be capturing."

It's as Joshua Porter, HubSpot's director of user experience, described in his interaction with Google Ventures' design studio. During all of their ideation sessions, they made sure that their ideas would remain:

> "Always be capturing" is about the habit of continuously recording the value from your conversation. For example: If you're talking about a new concept, you should be sketching it as you talk so your team has a shared understanding and an artifact of the conversation.[10]

In this way, the ideas that are flying between your consciousness and your voice and your colleagues' minds and their voices can be recorded, taken from the air, and put down on paper. The more artifacts created from a conversation, the more value you get out of a conversation. Since ideas are the start of strategy, we need to harvest them as well as possible.

One way is through the joys of analog. Having your creative space full of writing surfaces allows you to get ideas down on paper. As Porter suggests, if you're comparing two ideas, make a diagram of them since that will jog both your conceptual as well as spatial intelligence. As well, you can be liberal with sticky notes or notecards. This will let you form the component nodes of an idea to be assembled later.

But the digital can help you, too. As we found out in the birth of Indiana Jones, recording the transcript of a conversation allows for unforeseen value to arise later on. As well, you can use your smartphone to back up your analog assessments. Snap photos of the notecards and the whiteboards and upload them to a shared cloud account, allowing the team to access (and build on) those visualizations down the line. In this way, we can create a wealth of knowledge. Over our next two chapters, we will discuss how to put that knowledge into practice.

TAKEAWAYS

Ideas are the beginning of strategy. Just as we cannot have organizations without people, we cannot have strategy without ideas. As leaders, we need to be curators of both.

Ideas arise from curiosity. Experiences are the fuel of creativity. Curiosity is the thirst for new experiences. That passion can be systematized.

Idea generation can be structured. By being intentional about curiosity, we can refine it. By being rigorous about generating ideas, we can explicitly expand their values.

CHAPTER 9

BLUEPRINTING DECISIONS

". . . the proper correction is likely to be not the replacement
of one word or set of words by another but the replacement
of vague generality by definite statement."
—*E. B. White*[1]

DANIEL KAHNEMAN IS SOMETHING of a sage. He is a psychologist, yet he has won the Nobel Prize for Economics. Why? Because he's demonstrated through experiment and argument that humans are not entirely rational creatures. In fact, we're often quite irrational. We make decisions that aren't in our best interests, we act impulsively, we are blinded by unseen bias, and we take actions that aren't, to say the least, well evaluated. He recently put his several lifetimes' worth of insights into a book that anyone with an interest in their consciousness should read. *Thinking, Fast and Slow* is a book to be savored and lived with and returned to. (Your present authors hope to have a quarter of that effect.)

It is no surprise that wise people go to him for wisdom. One such occasion happened with Legg Mason Chief Investment Strategist Michael J. Mauboussin, who now tells the story with the distance of years. When they met, Mauboussin asked Kahneman what the one best way was for him to improve his decision-making. The psychologist's reply was to buy a notebook.

Your nearest composition notebook will do. What's it for? This is now your decision notebook, Mauboussin explained to the Motley Fool, the investment website:

> Whenever you're making a consequential decision . . . just take a moment to think, write down what you expect to happen, why you expect it to happen and then actually, and this is optional, but probably a great idea, is write down how you feel about the situation, both physically and even emotionally. Just, how do you feel?[2]

What do you get from such a pen-and-paper practice? Mauboussin explains that this mapping out of your decisions is a way of alleviating the happily hampering effects of hindsight bias—our tendency to view past events with a favorable tilt toward our noble selves. This has short-term benefits. It feels good to think you were right all along. But there are long-term negatives. If you make all your decisions in an unexamined fashion, then you won't learn from them very quickly.

The notebook acts as a record of your decisions. As you map decision after decision—and perhaps find yourself making mistake after mistake—you'll begin to recognize the elements of your identity, your various strategies, and the assets you're drawing upon for a given decision. Then, once you make a mistake, which will happen if you're stretching yourself in any way, you can go back to see where the misapprehension was. This is a very honest form of feedback that helps us spot our patterns of behavior and (in)decision. It is the kind of practice that helps us become better acquainted with the parts of ourselves we don't or can't acknowledge during the bustle of the decision-making time.

This is where we connect with the last chapter, where we took a broad approach to bringing as wide a range of experiences—and thus ideas—into our lives as possible. However, as we stated just a few pages ago, ideas are just the beginning of strategy. What are you to do once you've had an insight that could launch a company?

As we'll see with the story of the startup Orchestra, it's a matter of making informed decisions about strategy. We need to test that strategy to bring that idea a little closer to reality. We can do that by examining the interdependent causes and conditions that need to be brought together in order for an idea to find its home in the world as a product or service. By mapping these out, we can see what our assumptions are and where they might go wrong. And when they go wrong, we can find the incongruence between our perception of reality and the way it actually is. That mapping of the decision process is the center of our present chapter. Here we explore the art and craft of blueprinting.

MEETING THE BLUEPRINT

This mapping of decisions is not entirely new within the business world. In literature, white papers, and the rest, you might find mentions of technology architecture, process architectures, and other taxonomies. While useful to a point, these function as schematics of systems. It's like knowing all about your digestive or endocrinal system, which is great if you have a problem or solution particular to those domains. However, if you're acting with your whole body—as organizations tend to do with big-time decisions—you need a map that takes into account not just one or two of your organ groups but all of them and the way they interrelate. This is the promise of the enterprise blueprint: to draw lines around and between the different factors that contribute (or don't) to the success of a given idea as it moves into the world.

What this is, then, is a diagram of an action. And the body that's moving has many parts.

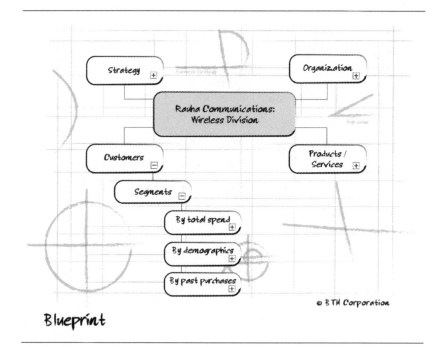

Blueprint

Identity

Whether deliberately designed or not, every organization has an identity. Both tangibly—that is, in the design and feel of the products and services it brings into the world—and intangibly—that is, the way people relate emotionally to the organization. This takes form in a number of ways. When we talk about branding, positioning, and differentiation, we're discussing organizational identity.

Western and Eastern psychological traditions make a distinction between the individual ego and the social ego. The individual ego is the way we think about ourselves, how we relate to our individual selves, and the gossip that tends to chatter about in our minds as we go through our days. Then there's the social ego, which is what other people think of us, how they regard us, and the feelings that we leave with them. If we extend this to an organization, the individual ego graphs on effectively to the organizational culture. That is, as we discussed earlier in the book, the way people relate to each other in the organization and especially to the idea of the "organization" itself. And that is the way the employee regards the brand of the organization they're working for.

We can see this intangible identity by evaluating the way we regard some of the major brands. The emotional connotation between a laptop made by Apple and one made by Dell is staggering—the former is sleek, understated, and emotionally aware, the latter vaguely robust and haplessly utilitarian. That cuts into high-end goods as well. Ferrari and Tesla both make cars that you might kill for, but only Tesla gives you the feeling that it's making the world a better place to live in.

Identity also rests in locations. Starbucks has a complex social ego, for it is more upmarket than a deli and more down-market than a posh café, and its ubiquity lends it an array of properties. The very cool may not wish to associate with something so common, while its pervasive penetration lends it a comforting familiarity. Your authors can't be the only ones who have regarded a Starbucks in an unfamiliar city as having a markedly maternal presence in our experience.

This social identity, of course, is most palpable in cases where you're interacting with people who represent the brand. Trader Joe's, the widely beloved grocery chain, makes a point of hiring creative, outgoing employees and pays them well (a practice we've argued for throughout this book). One of the positive outcomes of pro-social behavior of an organization is the pro-social interactions its employees have with customers—which is very, very good for the company's brand, its social identity, and its overall blueprint.

Strategy, then, is the struggle of taking this identity to market—a process we'll examine with one in-depth case study.

Reinventing the Mailbox

Have you ever had an insight that made you want to quit your job? What if you actually did it? Gentry Underwood had and did just that. His epiphany—and the multiple steps that brought it to its fruition—shows how the value you set out to create comes by different methods than you first assumed.[3]

Underwood is a prototypical example of a broadly experienced person. From his experience, he was able to generate subtle and profound insights—ones that can disrupt an industry or reform a basic electronic interaction, as we discussed in the previous chapter. Within thirty seconds of conversation with the man, one begins to appreciate that he is as quick-witted as he is sympathetic. His synapses fire fast, but that is only one of many admirable qualities.

Now getting deeper into his forties, Underwood tells with a certain flabbergasted amusement of Stanford letting him in for his undergraduate studies by virtue of his coding ability. He reveals how he would then find symbolic systems, a field at the intersection of philosophy, psychology, linguistics, and computer science. He talks of having a lifelong yearning to change things, which led him to work first as a therapist, though he'd soon pursue a PhD in social change at Vanderbilt. There, he would discover a dissatisfaction with academic life. It was too abstracted from the actual solving of problems.

Around this time, he learned that IDEO, the design-thinking consultancy, was looking to fill out their human factors team and was on the hunt for people with a mixture of social science and design. They needed people who had developed skills to study people and social groups but with enough of a design background to be a part of the design process. "My crazy mixed background of software design and sociology and ethnography was perfect for them," he says.

He'd be there from the summer of 2006 until the fall of 2010, where he led an internal team that designed and deployed an intranet system, one that, interestingly enough, would anticipate products like Yammer. He then started to consult other companies on designing their own intranet systems. But that was still not direct enough of an experience. As a consultant, he says, it's the difference between hitting balls at a driving range versus playing a proper round of golf. You may get to tee off, but you don't get to make the final putt.

And so, with that yearning for direct doing still simmering inside of him, he had a life-changing realization with Scott Cannon, who was then a team leader at Apple. During a Skype conversation, Underwood recalled the following:

> "The thing that got us to leave our jobs was the realization that people use email as a terrible to-do list. Everyone has stuff they need to do trapped in their inboxes, they feel overwhelmed, balls get dropped; it's a big mess. [There's] a lot of opportunity to make it a better experience. We said, 'What if we built a to-do list with the communication baked right into it? Can we skip that email step and help people to send tasks more directly?' Then people can free themselves of their inboxes."[4]

The result of that insight: Underwood and Cannon would cofound Orchestra in January 2011. The story of their finding that idea models the discussions of process and idea generation that we've been discussing throughout this book. Connections lie latent between unexamined fields. By finding those connections between things—like the psychological experience of using email on a mobile device and the mismatch that most mobile software has for that use case—extreme amounts of value can be uncovered. But not always immediately.

Underwood says Orchestra was formed with a founding promise: "to make tools that people actually want to use as opposed to tools that people are forced to use." And so, they soon launched Orchestra To-Do, a gorgeous app that allowed you to send and receive tasks from your contacts. It was a service Underwood and the team hoped would help people manage their tasks more directly and more socially, finally freeing people from their inboxes.

The app was launched in September 2011 and earned immediate accolades. The productivity blog Lifehacker named it the best to-do app for the iPhone, and Apple itself named it the productivity app of the year. Then it all fizzled out.

Underwood realized why when he was walking down the street in Palo Alto. His wife was supremely excited about the prospect of winning an auction on eBay, and she, who clearly had a vested interest in the success of Orchestra, emailed him the listings rather than sending it via her husband's app.

"Even our hardest core users still had tons of tasks trapped in their inbox," Underwood said in an interview. "We hand waved over a fundamental problem to our solution—unless the whole world made this switch, [then] best case, you're going to be managing two inboxes now. You weren't really going to be solving the problem."

In other words, Underwood and his team had found the right idea in identifying the right problem—that people were using email as a terrible to-do list. And, on an abstract level, they had discovered a suitable solution to make a productivity app with sharing built directly into the experience. But they had also made a mistake, one that, as we've discussed throughout our long conversation here, springs from a blind spot, an as-yet-unexamined ignorance.

Looking back at how Underwood and his team built the original Orchestra app, they suffered from a lack of context. That is, the way their product would fit into their users' lives, and especially how it would have to fit into their lives in order to retain an ongoing engagement, to be incorporated into the lives of their users. It's sort of like having an amazing pair of bright orange shoes (which, full disclosure, at least one of your authors has). They can be colorfully wonderful, but if they don't blend into your life, if they don't integrate into your preexisting behavioral patterns, they won't become part of your life. But after the fruitful failure of To-Do, Underwood and the Orchestra team set out to get to the soul of the task-email problem. To refine their answer, they would have to reframe their question.

"What would happen if we turned it on its head?" Underwood recalls asking. "What if instead of building a to-do list with the communication-like capabilities of email, what if we just transformed the inbox in which those tasks were already living into something with significantly better organization—a delightful experience. Could we build an inbox that gave people a different relationship with their mail?"

It was a question Underwood recalls that felt insane at the time. To essentially have all of your email be dumped into something like Orchestra To-Do, and you could then manage those embedded tasks with aplomb. But then another realization emerged.

"This seemed like an insane idea, building a to-do list that sucked in every email," he said, "and then we realized what we were really talking about was a rethinking of the email client itself." Their initial solution would then be turned on its head. "Instead of building a to-do list that worked like email," Underwood says, "we needed to transform your inbox, where all those tasks that are trapped in email live."

The result of that transformation opened up to the public in February 2013. Mailbox, a gesture-oriented email client organized around the way people deal with their email on their phone, as triage. In the same way an emergency room physician takes the most pressing cases first, when we open up our phones to check our mail, we're usually looking to see if there are any fires to be put out. What needs to be acted on now? What can be stored for later? What can be delegated? Upon studying this use case, Underwood and his team realized that the vocabulary of potential actions for mobile email was incomplete.

If you wanted to act immediately on something, you could reply. If you needed to delegate a task, you could forward the message. If you could simply get rid of the unwanted message, you could delete or archive it. But a piece was yet left incomplete: when you encounter a message that you don't want to deal with right now, but you know you'll have to tackle when you get back to your desk or later that night or the next morning or next week.

This is what you would call deferment, an organizational practice systematized (in an analog fashion) by David Allen and the Getting Things Done school of task management. You make separate buckets (often physical) for tasks to be taken care of in those respective blocks of time. But to manage all that analog organization is anxiety-provoking for people who have not built those organizational discipline skill sets, like at least one of your authors. So, as a good designer does, Underwood saw the opportunity to smooth out that rough edge. Swipe your finger across a message to the left, and you're prompted with eight forms of "snoozing" the message as you would an alarm clock: addressing it in a few hours, in the evening, the next morning, over the weekend, etc. In this way (and at its best), the app becomes like a personal assistant, an extension of yourself that you trust implicitly.

"We began to ask ourselves, how could we create a service that is reliable like the alarm clock is reliable, that didn't overpromise and didn't get cute, but instead simply began to establish a relationship with the user where more and more of those things that might have been living in their own head as unfinished loops," Underwood said in an interview. "[But instead, you] hand [the emails] off, and in being handed off, [they] could be forgotten about until the time that it was appropriate for it to be dealt with came. Then they could be paid attention to. That's the heart of this system, setting up that relationship."

If you've interacted with the app, you know that it is a beautiful experience, a "euphoric inbox," as Underwood would like to say. The app is quite simple. But, as the trend tends to be, these profoundly simple or obvious-after-you-meet-them solutions spring from deep insights.

Underwood's journey as a human led him to becoming an entrepreneur. And his journey as an entrepreneur fulfilled, at least from our vantage point, part of his journey as a human: to fulfill his lifelong need to fix problems directly.

And while Mailbox isn't the "solution" to email, it makes beautiful what was once ugly and makes resonant what was once repulsive. But that only came after a long train of personal experiences on Underwood's part (we didn't even touch on the time he spent doing field research as an ethnographer) that formed a multifaceted understanding of the way people work, which then informed the creation of Mailbox.

At its core, Mailbox represents a deep insight. We're tempted to call it app as poetry. As you would imagine, an app coming from someone with a deep involvement in human factors is deeply empathic. As our discussion has suggested, the greatest insights occur at intrapersonal and interpersonal levels. It's a matter of thinking with high degrees of contextual awareness. By joining an understanding of the ecosystem surrounding email and the system of email itself with deep comprehension of the way people interact with those systems when they're on their phones, Underwood and the Mailbox team were able to fulfill the founding promise of Orchestra: to create a tool that people wanted to use, rather than had to use.

And there's a happy ending, too. A month after Mailbox's launch, Orchestra was acquired by Dropbox for an estimated $100 million.[5] Such is the power of executing and then re-executing on an idea, one sprung from seeing how everything connects.

As Mailbox suggests, much of process and planning is the strange and serendipitous occurrences that happen as an idea finds its form in the world. You can have a penetrating insight—like an understanding of how people handle one of their primary modes of communication—but, with the intense unknowability of a volatile world such as ours, we're going to miss out on some aspect of the value that we're trying to create. Strangely enough, a great portion of planning, especially if we're opting for long-term growth over short-term profits, is to have a deep appreciation for how much we don't know (and how much we don't know we don't know).

CONCERNING ASSETS

Knowing that we will be wrong, how do we create the body of an organization in the right way? And how do we map it? When we're mapping out our decisions, we need to think of the "what" involved that will get us to the value we're trying to create. These are, in their many forms, our assets, the organs that form the fit, capable body of an organization—though they may lie outside of its walls, as we will soon discuss.

Presented bluntly, implicit within any decision is the question of "what do we need to get this done?" Put in business-ese, the question is "what assumptions need to prove true in order to have whatever plan we have in our heads make it into the world with some sort of efficacy?"

Blueprinting, then, is a sort of diagnostic of assumptions. We're trying to measure the inputs we need to get the outcomes we want. And the more granular we can be with that description, the easier we can see our inaccuracies and learn to spot them.

The greatest asset will always be people. Corporate culture might call us "human capital" or "talent" or "human resources," but we think we can just go with "people." Or, if you're feeling fancy, "persons." No product or service is made without a range of people. And the user, consumer, or customer on the other end, that's a person, too. When we consider any decision, we need to make sure we have the right people involved in order to make a plan reach its fruition. This is why, as we noted before, one of the primary responsibilities of a leader is to be a curator of talent. We want to hire the right people that fit our culture and help create spaces for them to find the right problems and solutions to create value for all the humans involved in the equation. So, when we're blueprinting a major decision, we should think of the group of people involved that will make it as amazing as possible, possibly using the cluster approach we proposed earlier.

The next asset is insight. It's become a truism that "entrepreneurs solve problems." But in order to solve a problem, you need to be able to first spot it. Before you can supply a useful answer, you need to supply the right question. The dustbin of history is filled with organizations that were answering the wrong questions—customers want a physical storage medium for movies, right?—so much of the work of any project is to be asking the right question, which is a subtle sort of knowledge. This is why we want to continually amass understanding. Finding the questions the world needs answered is an emergent process. We need to be always exposing ourselves to opportunity, which we discussed at length in the last chapter. The right insight can be powerful. The realization that people used email as a terrible to-do list motivated Gentry Underwood to start his own company. Though that insight didn't find its fulfillment until they moved on from Orchestra To-Do to Mailbox, which after all those long hours, allowed Orchestra to become an overnight success.

Then there's capital. It takes money to make money, the old saying goes. While not something to be worshiped, capital allows us to move with alacrity, to provide security to the people on our teams, and build the infrastructure we need to grow rapidly. As we have seen since the introduction, organizing our lives and our organizations around capital undermines the long-term potential of either. However, when used elegantly, capital can help us vault ahead of the competition. But be wary. Things usually cost more than one assumes. And be wary once again. Bringing in outside capital will come in exchange for one's autonomy—a phenomenon one of your authors knows quite well. But if you don't have enough capital for a long enough time, you don't have an organization.

An organization's plumbing and central heating is its infrastructure: the system of roots by which decisions are made and distributed among its people. This can take the form of software—any range of enterprise systems are included—to simply the way that decisions bubble up from data collected along the front lines or are mandated from leadership way up above. Being able to name the way your infrastructure affects your decision-making is perhaps as easy as biting your own teeth. It takes a lot of mindfulness to see how the organizational system will affect the organizational strategy and execution. This is another incentive, then, for having an experimental approach to organizational structure. If we try different clusters and other arrangements over time, we can begin to gain a sense of which form suits which format.

Last is the ecosystem. Just as any sort of value creation is contingent upon the people involved in its creation, any value is contingent upon its context. If the world isn't ready for your genius idea, your genius idea isn't going to catch on. Perhaps it's a matter of consumer taste. The Segway, once hyped as a world changer, has found its home for well-poised police officers and awkwardly balanced tourists. Or it could be a matter of broader infrastructure. One of the reasons the electric car (initially) had such a tough time catching on was the dearth of power stations. This is precisely why Tesla's determined installation of charging stations, though still in its infancy, is as great of an innovation as its Model S—and potentially more world-changing.

THE BORDERS OF THE BLUEPRINT

Often, the circumstances that allow a plan to reach its fruition are out of our control or unseen. This is what, we think, is suggested when people say "timing is everything." When we say timing, we really mean the way things are changing. And when those changes share the same trajectory, opportunity abounds.

But this doesn't always happen, as our dear maestro Leonardo's life evidences. Though he made many major works during his lifetime—this we know from the few that survive—he also left behind many incomplete works. We cannot know why he never finished his *Battle of Anghiari*, a landscape of war whose studies were so powerful that every young Italian artist worth his paints came to see it. Bramly, the biographer, contends that Leonardo made some mistake his painting technique would not allow him to correct, though we cannot say for certain.

The greatest example of how Leonardo's work fell apart (or, more accurately, melted) was with the *Cavallo*, the gigantic equestrian statue that Ludovico Sforza, the Duke of Milan, commissioned him to create. It was to be the largest equestrian statue in the world and a testament to the memory of the Duke's father, Francesco. Leonardo put immense effort into the project, starting, stopping, and returning. According to records, its model—at more than seven meters tall—was shown in honor of the betrothal of Bianca Maria Sforza in November 1493. He spent nearly two years researching how to cast the bronze monument. Leonardo was at his creative apex, and then something nonlinear happened. Charles the VIII, the king of France and commander of Europe's largest army, decided to invade Italy. As Bramly notes, the French had advanced artillery technology, prompting Italian technological advancement, which would require materials, like those for a horse, the metal for which would leave Leonardo in late 1494.[6]

Could Leonardo have completed the horse if he had blueprinted his process? All we can assert is a firm maybe. While Milan was prosperous at the time, peace was a fleeting thing in Europe, and the French were always on the other side of the Alps. If he'd considered that volatility a bit more—a theme we've discussed at length—then perhaps he would have completed the project. As Steve Jobs loved to say, "real artists ship." Blueprinting, then, is a way of ensuring that the shipping happens.

We need not be angst-ridden Renaissance masters to incorporate such things into our lives. We just need, whenever making a major decision, to sketch out the component parts. It would be wise to record our feelings at the moment as well, since anger primes people to make aggressive decisions and fear to make timid ones. There's a lot of talk about how important it is that we know ourselves. Certainly, there's been a cascade of it in this book you're presently holding. But relatively few practices help us see our blind spots.

We've spent a lot of time sketching out possible cures. One of those is meditation since it makes us more familiar with the movement of our minds. Another is the bond of partnership since close friends and colleagues can see things about us we would never see. Another is to allow ourselves to have a continuous dialogue with our present and future selves. Diagramming a decision—blueprinting, as we'll call it in an enterprise context—is a way of getting more intimate, more nuanced, and more rigorous in our approach to ourselves and to how we work in organizations.

TAKEAWAYS

We make better decisions having mapped them. When we make a decision, we tend to leave our understanding unexamined, whether as individuals or organizations. Mapping them out lets us have a more granular understanding of how we work.

Insights don't always find right answers in products the first time. While we might have the right insight—like the pain points surrounding the way we communicate—we might not have the right product.

We want to map our decisions with precision. The more precise we can get about the input included in a given decision, the richer the feedback we'll receive afterward.

CHAPTER 10

WHEN VALUE BECOMES
LONG TERM

*". . . if you're willing to invest on a seven-year time horizon,
you're now competing against a fraction of those people,
because very few companies are willing to do that."*
—*Jeff Bezos*[1]

THE BUSINESS WORLD IS a place full of euphemism. When we talk about innovation, we could be talking about many things, but probably some sort of incremental change. When we talk about disruption, we're probably talking about another sort of change, though less incremental in nature. But perhaps the most opaque and most crucial of all these thread-bare buzzwords is the phrase "to create value." What is value? What do we mean when we say that something is valuable? How about when a person is valuable to us? Are those two things the same? And what about products or companies?

In strictly economic terms, we can say value is about exchange, the price someone is willing to pay for a product—though that can hide the full picture. If, for instance, you're buying a shirt from a manufacturer whose supply chain pressures are so low it makes for unsafe working conditions in the developing world, then the price hides that greater, though less tangible, cost. As our friend, author, and self-professed value guru Nilofer Merchant would say, value can be a micro- or a macro-measure, a question of immediate transaction, or a whole package of exchange.

To get to the whole package, we need to do some digging. As usual, we can ground our understanding by getting to the root of the word. Value comes from the old French *valoir* or "be worth." What, then, is the function of the worth? Wealth, as we learned earlier, is stuff people want, and worth is closely linked to that. So, what do people want? At the core, people want what they think will enrich their lives, though that can be all sorts of things, whether or not they know it. This means that by making products and services, we make many sorts of interrelated values, though people may not realize it. The best products address these voiced and unvoiced potentials.

An aesthete among manufacturers, Apple has a deep understanding of such things. The *Forbes* writer Carmine Gallo captured as much, noting that if you walk into an Apple Store, you'll find the laptops arrayed on those beautiful blond wood tables to all have their screens tilted to a precise seventy-degree angle. It's just open enough for you to see that there's something going on in there but closed enough to obscure the desktop richness contained inside. This is by design. Why?

> ". . . to encourage customers to adjust the screen to their ideal viewing angle—in other words, to touch the computer!" Gallo writes. "It's also why all computers and iPads in the Apple Store are loaded with apps and software and connected to the Internet. Apple wants you to see the display for yourself and to experiment with apps and web sites to experience the power and performance of the devices."[2]

What Apple is trying to cultivate in its cozy confines of the Apple Store are ownership experiences, Gallo contends. This speaks to how much of value is unquantifiable, is not found within the price, and is emotional. What happens when you handle a product? You begin to get invested in it; you begin to see how it might integrate into your life (or not) and whether or not it will enrich your life. This is a much faster transfer of information than reading reviews or talking to friends about what laptop to get. You could even argue that it bypasses the logical system. This is the heart of long-term value creation over short-term profits. The more you as an individual or as an organization can become entrenched in others' lives as a source of benefit, the more you will be able to sustain it. However, as we have explored in the previous pages, this is not a single occurrence but rather a continuous process.

The more we can attend to the different facets of value, of the ways our individual lives and organizations can enrich the lives of others, the more deliberately we create it. From value creating, profits will emerge. That's the other side of value: the tangible, the bottom-line financials. When we're trying to create value for the long term—when we're trying to engineer organizations that sustainably innovate—we must take both the intangible and qualitative and the tangible or quantitative into account. This chapter, we hope, will provide that account.

We think part of the art of running a long-term organization is to recognize the relationship between the daily and the monthly, the quarterly and the yearly. Since we only get to experience things at one point in time, we tend to think now is the only moment and can only see how it relates to the future or the past upon reflection. There is a Greek proverb that "a society grows great when old men plant trees in whose shade they shall never sit." This aphorism doesn't perfectly graph onto our working lives—though surely if we're doing our very best work, it will carry over after we leave this place—but it does serve to help us see more clearly.

As we discussed earlier, positive acts within the present do not always have results immediately, even if they do make superb returns down the line. It's as if you as a parent miss all of your children's extracurricular events because you were toiling in the office versus if you attended those football games and dance recitals and other aspects of their early lives. The "returns" of family are not as immediate as burrowing into your work all night and getting a pat on the back from your manager the next day. But that doesn't mean they're not as valuable.

As we learned before, people aren't addicted to success. They're addicted to the validation that comes with success. We need to build in our psyches and in our organizations other mechanisms for validation; otherwise, that short-term-oriented, stuff-of-life-robbing system will remain entrenched. Such architecting was the concern of the previous section of this book, and we do hope it will be helpful in sculpting lives organized around meaning and growth—and from that, value.

That same subtle appreciation of intelligence attends to kids' sporting matches and to the experience of the person walking into a store to possibly interact with a product and the employees representing your brand. There is not an immediate return on the investment for piquing your potential customers' curiosity and courting them into playing with the product because there's no guarantee that the potential customer is going to make an immediate purchase. But that's not even what Apple is after, as Gallo himself observes. He walked inside the Apple Store with his daughters, and they immediately started playing on a display iPad, already associating Apple in their minds with fun and freedom. This is long-term—maybe even life long—stuff at work here. It is value created in the form of emotional content, brand loyalty, and product familiarization, all of which predict continued purchases, should the organization do its part and continue to innovate.

When asked about the entrepreneurs whose companies he's most interested in investing in, Bing Gordon, the Kleiner Perkins Caufield & Byers general partner, says that he's not looking for ten-week relationships; he's after ten-year relationships. Why? As he said to us, the company's first idea is probably going to fail at some point.[3] But with the right team, they'll be able to try another track. That's long-term value creation on a personal level, and it can be applied to organizational growth as well as relationships with members of the ecosystem and users.

As we discussed in chapter seven, the employees you have now are probably (certainly) going to leave at some point to pursue their own projects and otherwise self-development. That doesn't mean they've disappeared. They could, as one of your authors did, leave your gigantic corporation to start a consultancy and have that former employer become the first client. While life may be short, it is also long, as are the imprints we make inside people, both as individuals and as organizations. As Carl W. Buehner observed, people will forget what you said and forget what you did, but they will remember how you made them feel.[4]

In this way, value is a single event happening across many entities. It's kind of like Barbara Fredrickson, the positivity emotions researcher we discussed in chapter six, said about love—it's an event happening in two bodies, mirrored at many levels. When value is created, it resonates within everybody involved. A quality product, as we hope this book is, enriches the lives of the writers, the publishers, the readers, and members of the ecosystem that we can't even directly name, like the makers of e-reader or other people interested in holistic business or even the publications we already write for. The (hopeful) success of this humble little text you hold in your hands is something that radiates across many nodes of this strange, beautiful, and networked world of ours.

Interestingly, the values created by a product mirror the skills invested in it. It's the extension of Conway's Law that the internal systems of an organization are made manifest in its product. We can see that the internal lives of people are present in the products they make. Yes, the cool, comfortable, empathic simplicity of Steve Jobs and Jony Ive is certainly present in that seventy-degree tilt of the MacBook in your nearest Apple Store.

Value, then, is a kind of reciprocal relationship. It is a communication, in the same way your mouth creates a sound and your friend hears a word.

To take an example from the arts, a person masterful with the production of making sounds—that is, a musician—will be able to create great value when heard. In a less obvious fashion, the skills of a great manager will be present in the creation of their team. The crispness of the organization, if in alignment with the measured movement of progress among the individuals in the team, will show up in the form of the team's engagement, which will translate into an enthusiastically received product.

While each product is a single event—for physical products at least—the skills that created them are continuous. An Olympic sprinter, for instance, does not suddenly become slow after winning a medal. So much of continuous value creation is in the ongoing cultivation of skills. This can be seen across human endeavors, whether political, artistic, athletic, or commercial. To illustrate that, let us return to one of the few humans who embodied all these traditions.

LEONARDO'S EVER-GROWING VALUE

Leonardo da Vinci was a man of mottos. One of them was *saper vedere*, "to know how to see." The artist-engineer thought many people knew how to look, but few knew how to see, which reminds us of Truman Capote's admonishment that what Jack Kerouac did was typing, not writing.

How did Leonardo see? As Daniel Gelb reports, Leonardo's "Codex on the Flight of Birds" featured hyper-detailed observations about the movement of birds' wings that couldn't be confirmed until the invention of slow-motion film. To put it in the parlance of contemporary business-speak, that's one hell of a core competency. And it animated all of his work across the various domains he trod. For Leonardo, sight was the platform from which would spring the value that would erupt throughout his deeply lived life.

"Study of Hands" by Leonardo da Vinci.
Image is courtesy of the Art Renewal Center® www.artrenewal.org.

As is often the best case, Leonardo started developing his sight early in life. His sketch of the Tuscan countryside may have been the first landscape drawn in history (not bad for a twenty-one-year-old). His rigorous representationalism would help shift the blocky symbolism of the early Renaissance into the ethereal realism that he, Raphael, and Michelangelo would become immortalized by. Leonardo biographer Serge Bramly contends that the maestro's *Portrait of Ginevra de' Benci* was the first painted portrait to include the sitter's hands. The finished painting, now hanging in the National Gallery in Washington, D.C., has lost its bottom twenty centimeters and thus does not include anything of Ginevra below her bust. But studies for the painting show the gentle delicacy of the artist's observation—her right hand fingering at her bodice, her left resting at her stomach. It would require many more than a thousand words to capture the power of this preparatory picture, so let us defer to the artist himself:

"Give your figures an attitude that reveals the thoughts your characters have in their minds. Otherwise your work will not deserve praise."[5]

This speaks to the crucial nature of empathy, that is, a recognition of the human experience of whatever product we are using our skills to produce. Bramly contrasts the *Ginevra* with other portraits that were flat representations. Rather, what we have here is an image that embodies some ineffable attitude of the person being represented. And what is being represented? Bramly goes on to describe the image as a riddle, with the ambiguous sternness of the figure's face in juxtaposition with the delicate self-consciousness of the way she holds her hands. Perhaps this is a manifestation of a prodigiously modern woman in late fifteenth-century Florence, for she both wrote poetry and had poetry written about her, including sonnets from Lorenzo de' Medici (which, Bramly observes, was for her beauty as well as her refusal of courtship from a Venetian ambassador). What we have here is an image of softness and strength, independence and vulnerability. These are creative, united tensions that are as present in each of our lives today as they were 500 years ago.

This speaks to the fact that the work Leonardo created is the composite of many skills—that is, the platform he developed within himself and would continue to develop in a range of directions throughout his life. First, there is the keen attendance to natural forms, present in the photographic quality of the figure's features. Next is his sense for innovation, as the figure seems to blend into the background in previously unseen ways, an element of the sfumato he would continue to develop in his life.

And finally, there are the subtle fruits of introspection. While he was profoundly fascinated with the outside world, Leonardo also dwelt deeply within the environment of his own mental life. From these ponderings spring psychological passages among his notebooks and the deep interconnectedness he would return to again and again in his life. Just as we discussed in the first half of this book, intrapersonal knowledge breeds interpersonal knowledge. The contradictions and struggles and triumphs our artist delved into within himself—and the recognition of the way our interior spaces are made manifest in our external expressions—lend the figure the beauty of her precisely rendered tensions.

While having a bit of training in art history to arm one's self with sufficient vocabulary to describe it, the experience of taking in the image—especially those delicate, diametric hands—delivers the technical and emotional skills that the artist infused into the work. The value is multifaceted in the way the energy invested in it was multifaceted. And while we cannot say for certain how this artwork created value across the nodes of the Florentine network, we can assume that it esteemed the sitter and her house as well as that of the artist, who was in his mid-twenties at the time of painting. (Though now timeless, back then, he was an artist still establishing himself.) Just as the sprinter seeks to improve from a top performance and a hardware firm builds upon a market-shaping release, Leonardo would continue to invest in and draw from his virtuosity.

In the same way that a mature corporation will have many competencies developed along many axes (we can again return to P&G for an example), so did the maestro. As you'll recall, the strips that may be whitening your teeth this evening sprang from a collaboration between different arms of the world's largest consumer-goods company. It was a combination of laundry technology (bleach!), toothbrush-y institutional knowledge (what to do about the teeth), and canny ecological awareness (making a professional-grade product for dentists so as to not erode that crucial partnership).

If you'll recall chapter four, another organizational example comes from UPS and the platform-generating innovations they made. In the mid-1990s, the shipping giant realized their industry was maturing, so they would have to look elsewhere for growth. As has emerged as a theme, looking elsewhere included a need to look inward. The company had organized itself around becoming the best in shipping and, in so doing, had built a number of strengths within itself. It had become a technology company, an airline, and an insurance company, not to mention building the managerial and infrastructure capabilities to handle all those facets of shipping.

In the same way Leonardo developed in himself an expertise in observation in order to create value as a painter—an expertise that would be involved in the myriad works of the Renaissance man—so too UPS had trained talents within itself that could be applied elsewhere. When a PC manufacturer came to them for help with their logistics, the organization was able to apply a previously developed expertise in a novel setting. In the same way, strangely enough, the knowledge of the world Leonardo gained through his keen sight helped him throw masterful parties for dukes and duchesses.

For Leonardo and for UPS, it appears that the potential lying latent in the strengths they had developed was an emergent property, later discovered and seized upon. But we luckily have the benefit of reflecting upon their adventures and can be more deliberate in the way we view the relationship between an event of value creation (like making a painting or releasing a product) and the cumulative beneficial effects of platform building. Fascinatingly, the short-term and long-term forms of value tend to be quantifiable and unquantifiable, respectively. Leonardo was paid a handsome number of ducats for the "Masque of the Planets," we can be sure. But the fame he found as an engineer for his efforts would bring in more jobs and more ducats and more fame.

While it is indeed often subtle stuff, the nature of long-term growth is that it doesn't show up in a spreadsheet. Yet, the personal brand Leonardo slowly built was a key factor in growing his bottom line, as with businesses today. That's also the genius of the MacBook's tilt. No, you may not be making an immediate transaction, but you are building an emotional relationship with the brand, one that could, if you're a child playing with an iPad, become a lifelong part of your identity. This is very, very promising for Apple's bottom line.

Taken at a meta-level, Leonardo had a similar corporate-ness to the corpus of his work. He began as a painter, yes, and that painting trained him in observation. But that observation would ground his work as an engineer, architect, and anatomist. His dedicated observation has one of its most regular applications in flight, one of the master's lifelong preoccupations. Indeed, his faith in the power of study of life and the interconnectedness of things emboldened him to tackle the problem of flight with confidence. "The bird," he wrote in his notebook, "is an instrument function according to mathematical laws, and man has the power to reproduce an instrument like this with all its movements." Bramly the biographer notes that Leonardo developed a theory of flight based on the "force" of air, which, we could say, anticipated later insights into lift. Leonardo probably started out with toy-scale models of potential flying machines, though we don't know if he ever personally experimented with a human-sized device.

As we can see from the diverse sources of a Renaissance master and a shipping giant, value creation is a continuous conversation between inside and outside. As individuals and as organizations, we need to devotedly cultivate resources in ourselves, and these resources are sustainable when they find a home within the world. As we noted earlier in the chapter, to deliver products to the world—be they paintings or shipping services—we have to assemble the capabilities within us. But those capabilities do not evaporate after the product has shipped.

However, there must always be a recipient for what it is we want to create. If I make a gorgeous painting but don't make it available to the world, it is not valuable, you may say. Indeed, if I am treating art as a business, I would want to make something within the tastes of the buying public. When we think about building a platform and getting continuous value from the products we create, we're actually talking about a form of conversation between the producer and the consumer. The producer attends to the signals of the consumer and finds what they like next, even if they don't know it yet. Then, based upon the resources we've established in ourselves and the tastes broadcasted by them, we can make something that will delight them. This is how we nail the sweet spot of the adjacent possible.

TANGIBLE LONG-TERM VALUE

We now arrive where we started. At the beginning of our journey together, we talked about the mysterious obviousness of the best long-term performing companies of both startup and corporate size. Interestingly, the startups that were most likely to one day reach an IPO weren't ones organized around star power or bureaucracy or autocracy, but around commitment—where the members treated one another more like family than coworkers. (Upon being told of this research, one of your authors' best friends unhesitatingly replied, "You can't let family fail." We couldn't have said it better ourselves.) The research shows that pro-social behavior between individuals is, in fact, pro-business. Then, over the preceding chapters, we explored the different ways those bonds can be formed and why they are so powerful. We've recognized that organizations need to move with maximum velocity and that velocity is made possible by having a high degree of bandwidth between people—what you might call trust.

Then, of course, there was Shadoka's own research, which showed that sustained innovation predicted greater capital efficiency, better margins, more revenue growth, and more contained volatility. But sustained innovation is composed of a range of behaviors, like evolved organizational structure, collaborative behavior, and a concrete business blueprint. We then detangled these outcomes into their various behaviors. What kind of people working in what kind of way can do the individualistic yet collaborative and experimental yet structured path of sustained innovation? This path, we've found, is a personal and collective journey, requiring intra- and interpersonal skills—those which, with practice, we can begin to embody.

Lastly, there was the research of Alfred Rappaport, who has helped us see how "short-termism" has warped the behaviors of organizations and depleted their capacity for innovation. We then sought to find the intrapersonal skills that would help us free ourselves from short-termism—going as far as meditating on our own death and that of our organizations.

The relationship between short-term and long-term thinking has since been a recurring theme, one that we can see equally in our personal and professional lives. Cheating on your partner may sound like fun but will create suffering and affect your personal trajectory. If you're starting out in your career, taking a cozy job in a creativity-stifling environment might get you a quick payout but stunt your growth. And if you're a large organization, having a system of major annual rewards for executives creates an orientation toward acquiring those bonuses, rather than continually investing in this entity of an organization and its customers. In all of these cases, the quick hit certainly does feel good, but does it help us grow on various levels? This is the ethos we've attempted to describe—and live out.

EMBODYING VALUE

How can we apply the principles of continuous value creation to our individual lives? First, we need a healthy dose of self-awareness. We tend to get so focused on the work we're doing, the products we're creating, and the services we're providing that we don't realize what the work is doing to us. We don't realize the value it is building in us—at least until it's time to update the resume and court a new job.

When we say that a particular gig will be "good experience," we are embedding several meanings, one of them being that the experience will give us an opportunity to hone the skill sets that got us there in the first place. This is a useful way to think about career planning. If we're about long-term growth rather than short-term profit, we need to pick the clients, bosses, and organizations that allow us to continually build our skill sets and continue the momentum that we (and our ecosystem) have built thus far.

This is probably most obvious in cases of "breaking in." As we discussed before, even a young Leonardo has to do what every aspiring creative has to do—capture the attention of the powerful (or, today, a critical mass of people) and make the most of it. It was only after he designed the stagecraft, decoration, and illusions of the "Masque of the Planets" that Leonardo became esteemed as an engineer in Italy. The festivities were full of costumes and torches as stars and "half eggs" of the then-known solar system, if the court chroniclers are to be believed. While he would not reuse the bespoke effects of the event later in his life, he would continue to accumulate the social capital he gathered with the event, which would allow him to continue to grow his career as an engineer and artist.

What we need to attend to in our working lives, then, are similar inflection points—projects that can vault us across thresholds. If, as a manager, your team nails a project, then that creates value that radiates throughout the organization and into its ecosystem. And with that momentum, we can take on greater projects that stretch our skill sets, strengthening both our capabilities and our name.

Key to this strategizing, then, is identifying what our greatest assets are in the first place. In a way, Leonardo was lucky. His illegitimate birth drove him to the then-lowly profession of painting, which would train him in the keen observation that would define his career. Similarly, we need to be conscious of the handful of core skills that we're using across all of our various projects and be wise to find new applications. When asked about the resource he used the most, one executive interviewed in this book said that his contacts, what he uses between his company and his investing, and the relationships he builds are the most core of core assets.

And this, we think, brings us back to the opening of our journey. While we are doing business and inventing technologies and disrupting industries, all of that is an overlay on something intensely fundamental: the interactions we have within ourselves and with others. We as humans are fundamentally intra- and interpersonal, and so the depth of understanding that we have of ourselves and of others will be the skill that we use most throughout our working lives. The underlying architecture of our success, then, is the knowledge that everything connects.

TAKEAWAYS

Value is both immediate and long term. Any sort of transaction has short- and long-term consequences; the positive ones are called value. Short-term consequences will often be quantitative, long-term qualitative. A sustaining organization is conscious of both.

Value is symmetrical. The skills invested in a product or process by an organization are reciprocally experienced by the user. To experience a masterful performance, the performance must be done by a master.

To create value over the long term, build platforms. The most sustainable way to create value is to continually invest in our capabilities, both as individuals and organizations. The most core of these capabilities is the understanding we have of ourselves and others.

PART FOUR

PART FOUR

CHANGE, MORE ON MINDFULNESS, AND BUILDING RESILIENCY

THE ORIGINAL VERSION OF *Everything Connects* was expansive in its examination of the varied ways individuals and organizations need to pivot to adapt to a world characterized by ongoing change.

That recognition of the presence of dynamic change prompted this additional, new section. That's because so much has, in fact, changed that certain topics need to be added as well as revisited.

Chapter eleven opens the section by discussing just how much has changed and even become reinvented since we released the first edition of this book. From education to health care, our professional and personal lives have been upended and utterly transformed in the span of only a few years.

The chapter also emphasizes the enormous opportunities inherent in this level of change. Individuals have been empowered like never before. This affords us all the opportunity to leverage change in a variety of settings, from the health care patient as a consumer to how job seekers have reset the parameters by which they judge an attractive employment opportunity.

Chapter twelve mirrors the initial edition in that it discusses the value of mindfulness. But, while the original *Everything Connects* focused on the practice of meditation, this new section augments that with a discussion of mindfulness as everyday practice (one that doesn't have to involve sitting cross-legged on a meditation mat, focusing on a mantra). Given the level of change we've experienced, it seemed prudent to broaden the discussion of this core issue.

Chapter thirteen wraps up the new section with a wholly new topic: resilience. Again, what with the volatility and uncertainty sweeping change can often carry, the ability to develop and strengthen resiliency is as imperative as it has ever been. Hence, this new chapter covers strategies and mindsets with which to build resilience. As is the case with mindfulness, the flux of change has challenged us in many ways. Resilience is yet another implement in our personal toolboxes that can prove essential in our common journey toward happier, healthier, and more fulfilled lives.

CHAPTER 11

WHAT'S CHANGED?

"Every day the clock resets. Your wins don't matter. Your failures don't matter. Don't stress on what was, fight for what could be."
—Sean Higgins

WHAT'S CHANGED OVER THE past eight years?

A far easier question to answer is, What hasn't?

Since the first edition of *Everything Connects* was published in 2014, it's safe to say that virtually everything we do—be it how we live, work, play, or interact with one another—has undergone utter reinvention. Consider:

- Remote work has exploded. Some eight years back, despite the fact that nearly four million people worked at least part-time from home, remote work was still largely considered an aberration. It was an arrangement only applicable in special circumstances or seen as a special sort of "favor." By contrast, in 2021, nearly three-quarters of employees aged twenty-two to sixty-five say they work from home occasionally.[1]

- We stayed informed through different venues. By 2018, social media sites surpassed print newspapers as a news source for

Americans. One in five adults said they often get news from social media, slightly higher than the share who often did so from print newspapers (sixteen percent).[2]

- Health care has been made personal, 24/7. Eight years back, how many of us had even heard about telehealth, let alone actually interacted with a health care provider over the internet? Did you have a "wearable" back then that tracked your steps, heart rate, and other vital signs? Me neither.

- Education has also been transformed. In part fueled by the COVID-19 pandemic, virtual learning and education are now far more mainstream. But the change in education has by no means been limited to how we learn. In many ways, the very nature and purpose of learning are evolving. Not only do students want to embrace greater meaning in what they learn, but they also want to apply those learned skills in a moral, constructive framework.

One thing I did manage to do in the eight-year period was to write another book, this one entitled *LIFT*. This book explores the sweeping change and disruption brought about by the so-called "Fourth Industrial Revolution." This is characterized by the digital phenomenon that has been taking place since the middle of the last century, as well as the COVID-19 pandemic, climate change, and pervasive misinformation. Closely intertwined with the developments bulleted above and other forms of widespread change and intervention, these four drivers are upending every corner of society.

Moreover, not only are those drivers changing every aspect of our world, but they're doing so at a faster rate of change than we've ever experienced before. Unlike prior "revolutions," such as the First Industrial Revolution many years back that introduced widespread mechanized production, this fourth iteration isn't taking years or even months to take hold. Rather, its impact is both immediate and exponential. Not only is change taking place at a much faster rate than ever in our history, but it's also far more exponential. Phrased another way, what was new and cutting edge last week may be on the cutting-room floor of history this week in terms of relevance. The great ideas of yesterday are quickly being pushed aside by the arrival of even newer breakthroughs. And the momentum shows no signs of slowing down.

That challenges all of us to do more than simply keep up with the litany of ongoing change. In a world of explosive change and transformation, we are forced to rediscover, create value, and plan for our collective futures. If nothing else, through technology alone, we are all much more connected and at the same time empowered. We are positioned like never before to impact our world and those who share it with us.

That's an unprecedented call to action. The need for us to connect with the world by discovering our authentic selves couldn't be greater. We must not merely contribute all that we can to boost the common good but also create sustainable value in our interconnected world. And, on a fast-changing playing field, knowing one's innermost makeup from what we feel to what we believe and what we may prioritize has never been more valuable or, for that matter, essential.

What does this change entail? For one thing, it's empowering people with unprecedented levels of influence. By that, I mean the individual now enjoys widespread opportunity in any number of areas to impact their own life and future. Examples include:

- **Work.** In addition to the growing freedom of choosing where to physically work, employees, particularly younger ones, are choosing to prioritize issues other than simple financial compensation or career growth. These factors remain important, of course. But added to that list of desirable benefits is work they consider "meaningful" and that has a connection to a higher purpose or goal.

In effect, workers moving forward are no longer limited to doing well just for themselves. They want concomitant benefits for the world around them as well. For instance, in one study by the workspace software company Citrix, one emerging priority among job seekers is a reframing of how a company measures productivity. Rather than merely tallying quantity of output, more than four out of five employees cited the importance of the quality of the impact of their work in a more holistic sense. They want to see the value of their contribution to something more than just more widgets manufactured.[3] Employers who recognize this growing trend will have an inside track to attracting and retaining top-tier talent that embraces these newfound values.

- **Consumers.** The buying public currently has access to more forms of consumer information and guidance than all prior generations lumped together. But that empowerment goes well beyond what we buy at the store of our choosing. As "consumers" of all sorts—be it in education, health care, government, and other areas—individuals are now positioned to have a much greater role in deciding what they want and how they wish to receive it. Further, they want the company with whom they do business to espouse values that they embrace as well (community involvement, climate awareness, and commitment to the total well-being of its employees, among others). Further, as an analysis by global consulting concern Accenture summarizes, "[Reimagined consumers] are ready to abandon brands that don't support their reimagined values. And pay more to those that do."[4]

- **Education.** While one of the more visible forms of change in how we learn has been the growth of virtual and remote learning (spurred to a large degree by the COVID-19 pandemic), education is also shifting its focus to prioritize different skills and learning.

One such area has to do with the value of "soft skills" or so-called "people skills" such as intelligence, empathy, confidence, and integrity. In an era where technology and robotic work are increasingly moving to the forefront, the ability to empathize with and relate to others is becoming all the more valuable. We must maintain a balance between technical efficiency and growth and the insight and perspective only a human can provide.

- **Health care.** As with other areas defined at least in part by the presence of consumers, health care is tracking the path of other areas in prioritizing patient involvement and input into medical decision-making. That will be made all the more effective through a growing emphasis on proactive and predictive health care, essentially shifting the health care model away from a focus exclusively on cures to one that anticipates and prevents disease. That shifting focus will impact much more than the individual. A study published by the National Institutes of Health examines the more pervasive benefit to what it refers to as "longitudinal wellness"—improving proactive health care and treatment for entire populations and geographic areas.[5]

These and other forms of transformational change can be boiled down to the essential importance of developing emotional intelligence. As I describe it in *LIFT*, that refers to the capacity to be keenly aware of your own emotions and the impact they can have on personal or professional relationships. Emotional intelligence recognizes the essential and constantly changing nature of what's construed as valuable. Emotional intelligence embraces the power and role of community—inspiring yourself and others to pursue meaningful and beneficial change. Emotional intelligence moves away from an exclusive emphasis on the here and now to long-term ramifications and consequences. It's a vision for today as well as tomorrow.

With so much more on our collective plates now in the mere eight years since *Everything Connects* was first published, we are all called to action to make the most of the enormous opportunities that such widespread change and evolution afford us. Everything is changing and transforming, and it's all going to come at us faster and faster. It's essential we react accordingly, with open minds and an eagerness to capture the opportunity widespread and dynamic change presents every one of us.

TAKEAWAYS

Recognize the change. The more we understand and, in a sense, appreciate the widespread, dynamic changes occurring, the better positioned we are to leverage those changes to our advantage rather than allowing those changes to dictate how we live.

Hiring? Know that applicants' attitudes have shifted. Employers, organizations, and companies need to understand that the priorities of job applicants are no longer limited to a focus on just salaries and benefits. Workers want to believe in a company's mission and their capacity to contribute to that vision.

Health care: prior, not after. Patients are now very much in the role of empowered consumers. They increasingly expect their health care providers to offer proactive health care programs and guidance, not just the capacity to treat illness and disease.

CHAPTER 12

MINDFULNESS

*"Drink your tea slowly and reverently, as if it is the axis on which
the world earth revolves—slowly, evenly, without rushing toward
the future. Live the actual moment. Only this moment is life."*
—*Thich Nhat Hanh*

IN THE FIRST EDITION of *Everything Connects,* I focused on the concept
of mindfulness with a rather specific focus—meditation and the varied
ways it can help improve us, our work, and how we interact with others.

But it's essential to point out that mindfulness encompasses much
more than time spent on a meditation mat.

And it can all start with a single breath.

Put simply, and as the name suggests, mindfulness is the ability to
be fully present. By that, I mean a person who consciously works at
being fully aware of where they are and what they're doing in the current
moment. That also suggests a focus away from thinking about the past or
what might occur in the future and, instead, being as fully locked as possible on what is taking place right now.

In that regard, there's a good deal of crossover between mindfulness
meditation and what might be called "everyday mindfulness." Both involve
directing our attention toward the immediacy of experience. In the case

of meditation, that can mean focusing ourselves on a particular point of focus—the breath, for instance, or a mantra we repeat over and over.

But non-meditative mindfulness doesn't limit that activity to a specific timeframe. Rather, it's something of an ongoing exercise to help rein in rampant, scattered thinking; when we do this, we become that much more present in the moment. The practice of mindfulness allows us to be more fully engaged and helps us make better decisions. Overall, this helps us to be happier and more connected to the moment at hand.

In fact, mindfulness shouldn't be viewed as some sort of exotic process or a "different" way to think and behave. We all naturally possess the capacity to be more present and fully engaged. It's built into us. To that end, think back to a time or an experience—a piece of music, for example, or a project or piece of work that utterly engaged you—that was so consuming that your attention and awareness were completely locked in.

Further, try to remember the outcome of that particular experience. Chances are good it was positive. That's because the depth of mindfulness can completely involve your intellect and attention—a powerful formula for great things. There's a reason people often speak of athletes performing at their very best as being "in the zone." That's just another way of identifying mindfulness, albeit at a very high, specific level.

It's also important to bear in mind that the experience of mindfulness isn't always positive. Rather, it's a way of accepting and being fully honest with ourselves. If, for example, we're trying to be mindful about a particular problem or challenge, mindfulness doesn't simply "make things better." Instead, mindfulness simply encourages us to focus on what is there, warts and all.

That sort of internal candor also allows us to respond more effectively to many different situations. By encouraging both attention and acceptance, mindfulness lets us keep matters in a better perspective. We can be less prone to feeling overwhelmed, overreacting, and making snap decisions. Further, mindfulness implicitly encourages us to be less judgmental in our thinking. Again, things are no longer seen exclusively as right or wrong—they just are.

Additionally, we do not have to take the benefits of mindfulness on faith alone. Extensive research has documented how mindfulness can work for us in any number of ways:

- Decreased depression and anxiety levels

- Improved immune function

- Better heart health, including lowered blood pressure

- Improved sleep

- Greater creativity

Not to downplay their significance, but the benefits go beyond happier, healthier lives.

Corporate executives and others in positions of leadership are increasingly pursuing formal mindfulness training to better manage stress and, in so doing, make better, more thoughtful decisions. As Harvard Business School professor Bill George points out in a piece that originally appeared in the *Huffington Post*, the practice of mindfulness allows leaders in varied capacities to hone their focus to "ensure the important issues are taking precedence over immediate pressures."[1]

As further evidence of the fast-growing synergy that characterizes how everything connects, mindfulness is also increasingly employed by health care professionals as a proactive measure to reduce stress and other mental health issues. As detailed in a paper published by the American Psychological Association, mindfulness can not only improve patient outcomes in therapy, but the practice of meditation can also help mental health professionals perform their duties more effectively and with lowered levels of stress.[2]

Just as valuable, while a mindfulness practice can include formal, scheduled meditation sessions, there are many other ways to incorporate mindfulness into our daily lives. For instance, one easy-to-learn technique that can be practiced any time of the day or night goes by the acronym of S.T.O.P. This breaks down as

- S—Stop what you're doing, if only for a moment.

- T—Take a breath. Look to breathe slowly and completely.

- O—Observe. How do you feel? What are you thinking about right now at this very moment in time?

- P—Proceed. Return to what you were doing. At the same time, take notice of how you approached the activity. Do you feel refreshed? Can you look at what you were doing from a different perspective?

That's all there is to it. The S.T.O.P. methodology affords you a break during which you can reconnect with yourself and what's going on around you. Scientific estimates hold that some ninety-five percent of our behavior derives from an autopilot dynamic—essentially neurological "shortcuts" that our thinking automatically defers to. S.T.O.P. is one simple way in which mindfulness can short-circuit ingrained, knee-jerk thinking and reactions. Instead, we reconnect ourselves with what's happening at the moment, not what we think might be happening.

There are any number of other ways to incorporate mindfulness into our daily routine and behavior. For instance, during the COVID-19 pandemic, we were all told repeatedly to wash our hands thoroughly and on a regular basis. While valuable on a physical basis alone, that practice also affords us the opportunity to practice mindfulness for a brief period. Rather than simply washing your hands without a thought in mind, consider the value of what you're doing. What is your intention in washing your hands? Pay attention to the movement of your hands in their interplay with soap and water. And, if a thought comes into your mind that diverts your attention away from the experience, acknowledge it, then return to a focus on the business of cleaning your hands.

Mindfulness can be particularly effective when practiced in the earliest parts of your day. One way to do that is to set your intention for the day shortly after waking up. What do you hope to achieve? How do you hope to achieve it? Just as important, what are you going to do today to benefit yourself? Are you going to treat yourself with understanding and empathy? Further, whatever your intention, are you going to check in at regular intervals throughout the day to see how closely your day is aligning with your stated goals?

The practice of setting your daily intention works much in the same way as other mindfulness practices and exercises. It aligns our subconscious (where our thinking and behavior really start) with conscious activity. By linking a specific objective to the ongoing function of our minds, we move our goals to the forefront of our daily activities. That can mean better decision-making, fewer knee-jerk reactions, and a greater sense of empathy and connection with others.

Other opportunities for mindfulness are everywhere. For instance, when eating a meal, take the time to slow down, breathe, and savor every bite and texture of your food. Pay attention to your body as you continue the meal. Focus on your level of hunger. If you're no longer craving more food, mindfulness can be a powerful diet aid in reminding yourself when you've truly had enough to eat. Additionally, take into consideration those foods you truly enjoy and those less appealing. Prioritize meals with food that you really like and consider alternatives rather than eating something out of boredom or "just because it's there."

Take a similar approach to working out and exercising. Before you begin, set your intention for that particular session. What do you want to gain from this particular workout? After taking sufficient time to warm up, monitor your breathing and your body as you exercise. If all feels good, think about boosting the intensity a bit. Check in with how you feel as you ramp up your efforts. Don't just throw the brakes on at the end of your workout. Take the time to slow down and cool off. Pay attention to the way your body feels as your heart rate and breathing begin to slow down.

Lastly, give some thought to making a conscious effort to focus on one thing or activity at a time. Although many of us have been led to embrace the productivity of multitasking, the reality is not only can that kick auto-pilot thinking into high gear, but in so doing, we may inadvertently fail to give each project or responsibility the time and attention it needs. Being mindful and taking things a step at a time lets us enjoy our activities that much more while at the same time helping to ensure greater success in whatever we happen to be doing.

Needless to say, there are many more aspects and characteristics of mindfulness than can be addressed in a single chapter of a book. Accordingly, if you'd like to find out more about mindfulness—including strategies with which to start a mindfulness practice—one great place to start is the website mindful.org. There, you can find a variety of resources to investigate and adopt whatever aspects of mindfulness may appeal to you, including meditation instructions, magazines and periodicals on the subject, and an online community of like-minded individuals.

Additionally, should you wish to pursue individual instruction and coaching, mindful.org offers a directory of mindfulness teachers. You can browse according to location, professional background, approach, areas of expertise, and other criteria. Many people interested in mindfulness have found that a one-on-one relationship with an experienced professional can be invaluable in learning the essentials of mindfulness, overcoming obstacles, and building confidence in a mindfulness practice.

In a constantly changing and reinvented world where everything is increasingly connected on many levels, mindfulness should no longer be seen as a New Age fad or the latest feel-good practice that comes and goes with the wind. Instead, it's becoming increasingly evident that mindfulness is an essential practice in a shifting environment that mandates careful thought, flexibility, and an openness to consider new things. Whether you embrace mindfulness through meditation, everyday activities, or a combination of the two, mindfulness can position you—personally as well as professionally—to make the most of the opportunities afforded by widespread, ongoing change.

TAKEAWAYS

Mindfulness can be more than meditation. Meditation is an important component of mindfulness. But mindfulness can also be practiced by taking steps to slow down and direct your focus toward the immediacy of the moment, rather than allowing the mind to race uncontrollably.

One Strategy: S.T.O.P. A technique that allows for mindfulness practice on the fly is known by the acronym S.T.O.P. This means: S—Stop what you're doing; T—Take a breath; O—Observe; P—Proceed. Even a few moments applying this strategy can bolster clearer thinking and a calmer demeanor and outlook.

Do it every day. Mindfulness is a powerful tool, but only if it's practiced on a consistent basis. Try to make time for mindfulness every day, even if it's only a few moments here and there to stop what you're doing and observe your breath.

CHAPTER 13

RESILIENCY

"Another way to be prepared is to think negatively. Yes, I'm a great optimist. But, when trying to make a decision, I often think of the worst-case scenario. I call it 'the eaten by wolves factor.' If I do something, what's the most terrible thing that could happen? Would I be eaten by wolves? One thing that makes it possible to be an optimist, is if you have a contingency plan for when all hell breaks loose. There are a lot of things I don't worry about, because I have a plan in place if they do."
—The Last Lecture *by Randy Pausch*

IT WOULD BE EASY to say that many of us would struggle to imagine a time when our inner strength and resiliency were tested to the degree they have been in the last few years.

I said it would be easy, although not necessarily accurate. Those still alive having endured World War II, for instance, could argue with a fair degree of justification that several years in a world war against a highly armed madman was exceedingly taxing. I'm certainly not here to argue that point.

But, from another perspective, the events over the past three years or so certainly could not be categorized as the proverbial walk in the park. First has been the onset of the COVID-19 pandemic. Then, when we were all convinced we had come out on the other side, variants cropped up, prolonging widespread anxiety. Add to that the politicization of what should be addressed simply as a public health issue, and this has further exacerbated the tension of a situation that was already sufficiently nerve-racking.

An additional component is the prevalent uncertainty surrounding the pandemic. Are the vaccines effective? If so, how many should a person receive? To what extent do they work? Should we be masked, and with what sort of mask? Can we gather safely with family and friends? Under what conditions and restrictions? And on and on.

Then there are events outside the realm of public health, such as the January 6th, 2021, attack and attempted coup of the United States' electoral process and democratic transfer of power, which had proceeded largely unscathed since the country was founded. The subsequent drawnout investigation has been punctuated by the frustrating slowness with which authorities have pursued not just the rioters themselves but those who, as it has become increasingly evident, planned the uprising and urged on those who took part. The result has been anxiety as to whether the events of January 6th presaged repeated attempts to violently disrupt the legitimate democratic process.

Without resorting to pointless discussion as to who in history has endured more, it's nonetheless safe to say that the past several years have tested our inner strength in numerous ways. Boiled down to one component, our resiliency and ability to repeatedly bounce back from horror, disappointment, and disgust have undoubtedly been tested to their fullest extent.

As I document in my book *LIFT*, a period of time characterized by change and uncertainty can present enormous opportunities for those capable of seeing more than ongoing discouragement. And, with regard to the situation as things exist today, we all have an enormous opportunity to strengthen and, if need be, restore our collective resiliency.

In another one of my books, *Survive to Thrive*, I describe resilience as the capacity to rebound from a host of challenges and problems, including illness, depression, and personal and professional setbacks, just to name a few. Rather than being a characteristic that we naturally possess, resilience is also something we can develop over time. And, just as important and as evidenced by the times in which we are now living, it's also a skill that we can revive.

In the remaining portion of this chapter, I'm going to offer some strategies with which we can all do just that.

It goes without saying, it's essential we all work to strengthen our sense of resilience. As my book's title hints, being resilient is critical to surviving. But, perhaps even more important, it's critical to the capacity to thrive. Lacking the strength to continually push forward in pursuit of better outcomes and lives, our professional and personal lives and those we care about would undoubtedly suffer.

There are a number of other practical benefits to being resilient. Greater resilience not only contributes to greater academic achievement by students, but resilient individuals also have fewer absences from work and are less vulnerable to substance abuse. Greater resilience has also been linked to better overall physical health and decreased mortality.[1]

It can also lead to greater professional achievement. As I discuss in *Survive to Thrive*, entrepreneur Julie Wainwright credits the resilience from one failed company—Pets.com—and a failed marriage to her subsequent successes: "I just got on with it and never gave the [negative aspects] another thought."[2]

Nor does it have to be solely a matter of faith, although that's a critical component for many. By examining the various factors involved in stressful situations and our ability to deal with them, we can come to understand and embrace a more systematic approach to building and strengthening our resilience, both as individuals and a community.

One of the first steps to fostering a strong sense of resiliency is to get past the feeling that it's somehow bad or unhealthy to be gripped with feelings of helplessness. Nothing could be further from the truth. For one thing, mental health experts point out that discouragement and resilience can take place in our minds at the same time. Phrased another way, just as you're feeling the lowest and most distraught imaginable, you may also well be building a solid sense of resilience. Sometimes you have to hit what feels like rock bottom to begin making your way back toward the surface.

That ties in with another concept I touched on earlier. It's during times when life seems the most challenging and even desperate that we can best leverage the opportunity to build resilience. You've no doubt heard of people presented with a dire health condition who say it proved a watershed moment in their ability to recapture a sense of resilience. It should be noted, this is sustained long after the health issue has been addressed and a person is able to resume their regular life. Approaching challenging times and situations with a focus on opportunity rather than a sense of utter helplessness can be fertile ground on which to rebuild resilience.

Additionally, don't make the mistake of overlooking constructive memory. By that, I mean recalling prior times and circumstances where things may have looked bleak, but it all turned out reasonably well. In times of stress, we can all fall victim to the idea that we've never been through anything like this before, and bad outcomes are almost a certainty. Although comparing one challenging period with another is a fool's errand, the fact remains we've all endured challenges, crises, and even out-and-out tragedies. We've usually come out on the other side before, so there's no viable reason to conclude now is going to be any different.

Touching on a topic addressed in the prior chapter, empathy can also play a valuable role in strengthening our sense of resiliency. During periods of stress and even hopelessness, it's easy and natural to feel unduly singular—as if you're the only one going through all this worry and uncertainty. Even though that's an utterly preposterous conclusion, we all have a tendency to do it.

On the other hand, looking at the situation with empathy helps us break away from that destructive sense of isolation. By recognizing this and directing more of our thoughts and actions outward—by helping others with their own feelings of fear and anxiety, for instance—we don't allow our negative emotions to needlessly fester. It's a reminder that, however clichéd the expression, we're all in this together. That alone can temper a feeling of singular despair.

Taking the issue of empathy a step further, trying to weather crises and challenging circumstances on your own can be a treacherous journey with a good chance of failure. Instead, akin to the mindfulness practice of considering others, make certain to build strong connections, both personally and professionally, with others. Sharing your feelings and reactions and listening to others with similar experiences can not only bolster an uplifting sense of community, but you also may discover new and effective coping strategies that have worked for other people. Share both the strength and feedback support groups of all sorts can offer.

Referencing another issue raised earlier, emotional intelligence and mindfulness can also be powerful weapons in defusing runaway despair and, in turn, help one build a greater sense of resilience. The core principles and practices of mindfulness—working to restore a focus on the moment at hand and preventing our minds from automatic, frenetic dashes into negative and even destructive emotions—can be exceedingly effective in pulling us back and restoring a sense of perspective. As I discussed, even a few moments of deep breathing can be enough to reprogram our minds back toward a healthier, more constructive outlook.

Moreover, take time to savor those moments and experiences that are joyful and uplifting. It's rare—if not completely unheard of—to endure a period of time when simply nothing goes well. Instead, it can be helpful to pay particular attention to events and occasions that run counter to what seems to be a one-way flow of disappointment and setbacks. Even something as simple as gathering family and friends to watch a classic movie you all enjoy can break a prevailing negative mindset and, further, remind us that embracing such challenges as a group is not only fun but powerfully therapeutic.

One strategy used to begin collecting joyful and rewarding moments and experiences is to connect with a higher purpose. For some, that may translate to a religious practice—a well-established, effective pursuit. But connecting with a sense of purpose doesn't have to be exclusively of a spiritual nature. For instance, volunteering can prove a wonderful means of finding joy, particularly in times of pervasive hardship and uncertainty. Not only can that offer rewarding relationships and experiences, but also the feeling of simply "doing something" rather than just wallowing in fear and anxiety can be equally powerful. Instead of just sitting back and "taking it," you feel as though you're actively pursuing a happier state of mind on a proactive level.

Connecting with a greater sense of purpose doesn't have to be limited to spiritual pursuits or how we choose to fill our spare time. Your professional life also affords the opportunity to feel a part of something greater than yourself, however that might manifest. In my book *LIFT*, I discuss at length how a deeper sense of meaning is becoming an increasingly important criterion for job seekers, particularly younger ones. For many, finding the ideal job is no longer a matter of the fattest paycheck or a generous benefits package. They truly want to know their work means something. No matter the professional or personal setting, that's a solid lead to emulate.

Another issue I stress in *LIFT* is the importance of dealing with struggle and failure in the most constructive manner possible. For far too many of us and for far too long, the prevailing attitude has been one of "come home with your shield or on it." In other words, either you succeed, or you fail. There is no gray area in between or other way of looking at it short of a simple question of winning or losing.

That may be "traditional" for lack of any other way to phrase it, but it's not the healthiest approach, particularly in times and situations when so-called success or failure's ramifications can seem magnified. Instead, look at each situation as an opportunity to learn. If you succeed, wonderful—break down what went well and look to replicate that in the future. On the other hand, approach so-called "failure" with a far more open mind. Try not to focus exclusively on what may have caused unsatisfying results. Instead, pay attention as well to what did work. Look at the experience as a step toward better outcomes in the future. The more you learn about any experience—warts and all—the better positioned you will be to apply that knowledge effectively moving forward.

Another story from my book *Survive to Thrive* personifies this. Brent Daily's professional credentials were excellent—an MBA from Stanford's Graduate School of Business—but when he joined an intriguing startup, he found his work style often clashed with others in the company. Eventually, he was diagnosed with clinical depression, traced to his experience at the company, which he had left. Just as destructive, he began to question himself, wondering if there was any place where he could work happily and successfully.

He ultimately found it in a company of his own creation—Round-Pegg, a firm focused on helping companies hire, develop, and engage employees in alignment with the desired company culture. In effect, the company's mission he successfully brought to life was to help others avoid the same fate he had himself experienced.

"Failure is a funny thing in that it doesn't really exist if [you] look through the right light," he said. "If you put in your best and make the best decisions you can, is it really failing if it doesn't work out?"

Perhaps as valuable as anything else you can do, believe in yourself, as Daily was ultimately able to do. Tell yourself you're up to the challenge of coping with whatever may come your way. Research has shown that self-esteem can be pivotal in dealing with stress and the capacity to bounce back from setbacks and disappointment. Once more, tap your memory for times in the past when you overcame significant challenges and obstacles. The fact that such memories are real is tangible proof that you're up to meeting whatever may come your way—even if you stumble and fall on occasion.

Pay attention to what your inner voice might be telling you. If you hear a negative comment like "What's the point?" or "I'm just not up to doing this," note them and consider replacing them with something more positive and constructive. Always remember that your thoughts are not reality. They are interpretive, reflective, and analytic but not based in the genuine here and now. Whether they actually do occur or not is anything but a foregone conclusion.

Lastly, make building resilience a habit. Very few things of genuine worth are achieved overnight, and a strong sense of resilience is no exception. Whether it's through mindfulness, meditation, or some of the strategies detailed earlier in this book, approach resiliency as a daily project that needs ongoing connection to grow and flourish. Understanding and commitment are the keys to fostering resilience and working to strengthen this invaluable characteristic. Stick with it, and the results will likely speak for themselves.

TAKEAWAYS

As critical as it's ever been. Given all the uncertainty and volatility present in the world today, resilience is particularly critical to navigating any number of environments, circumstances, and situations. This doesn't dismiss what prior generations have had to overcome. In fact, knowing that they did overcome can help build resiliency and confidence in us that we can and will do the same.

It can be learned. Although some people can be described as naturally resilient, a strong sense of resiliency can be developed and strengthened in everyone. If nothing else, watch for negative, discouraging thoughts and look to recraft them in a more positive manner.

Leverage empathy. As the old saying goes, we are all in this together. Constantly recognizing that reality and being empathetic to the challenges and difficulties faced by others can be a powerful strategy to foster and nurture your own sense of resilience.

EPILOGUE

WALKING DOWN A TREE-LINED street on a cool Brooklyn night, we found ourselves with a friend from a former life. It was Michael, the lyric-tongued, shaved-headed meditator we met in the courtyard of a Tibetan monastery in Kathmandu. The conversation looped in on itself in the way re-meetings do. We spoke of the way things end and, in ending, don't end.

"Think about what happens," our friend, the wandering yogi, said. "If what we really are is bundles of energy, if our thoughts are a part of us, then when people and places come into our minds again and again, they really are a part of our mental lives, and therefore part of our selves."

Such a thing is powerful to hear, especially only days after a relationship comes to an end, when the person we once related to, who was once physically next to us, is now known only in the mind. There are only memories of the smiles, the glances, the way that when she's thinking deeply, she sweeps her hair to one side. When a relationship ends, a physical presence may be gone, but a total presence is not. In the same way, a place once visited stays with us when we return home. We are what we've eaten. We are what we've experienced: the places, people, and other loves with whom we've lived.

When a book is good, as we hope this one is, we begin to live with it, stealing into its pages when waiting in line or making a commute. We rely on its touch when we need some assurance. And, in time, we return to it, revisiting the dog-eared pages months later. In doing so, we meet the person we were back then.

We hope to have earned a few of those dog-ears over the past few pages. Although it's not that our relationship is ending—this is not a breakup, dear reader—it is time for our relationship to transform. If you've made it this far, to the very last pages, we thank you for your time and energy and effort, for your willingness to meet us where we are. We thank you for offering up the increasingly scarce resource of reading time to go on this walk with the two of us and the dozens of highly realized humans who have appeared in this odyssey.

This brings us back to the sense of journey, to the sense of purpose. When we were discussing the arc of collaboration—how it is both an individual, lonely pursuit and a collective, companionable one—we brought to mind the ideas of Joseph Campbell, the comparative mythologist whose life's work showed that the religious traditions of the world are not separate stars but are part of a greater constellation.

One of Campbell's most essential insights was that religions (and literature) have a story structure universal to all of them—that of the hero and the journey. Reduced to its most basic elements, the hero is often an orphan or is orphaned in the course of the story and must go in search of an identity. In doing so, they will venture into the wilderness to find something of use to the people of the world and bring it back to them. A Holy Grail in its many guises. We hope that this book, and the many threads that have been woven here, have helped you search inside your personal and organizational wildernesses for grails you had not yet known. May you bring them into your life and those of your family, friends, and colleagues.

In this way, with our walk ending, we hope to remain a part of your life, a firefly lighting within your memory, a signal pointing to the implicit connections underlying the way you engage with your consciousness and that of others. We admit the title for this book is a touch grandiose when you first hear it, but upon reflection, it's rather obvious, even humble. Of course, it all connects.

In *A Path with Heart*, Jack Kornfield relates an old Jewish story that we think will make a suitable final scene. One hundred fifty years ago, there was a young rabbi in New York who was hungry in all the right ways: to meet God, to serve his people, to deeply know himself. One could say that his religiosity was an ambitious one.

As he was growing up and growing into the rabbinical world of America, he kept hearing about a master teacher in the Old World. He was an older rabbi living in St. Petersburg, Russia, with jarring insights into the Talmudic tradition. A mentor in Manhattan gave the young man the master's address, and with some trepidation, he wrote to him, asking about his journeys in the faith, the lineage of the Jewish people, and the symbolic meaning of ritual.

The master replied with grace and sagacity, showing a wealth of lived experience. They wrote to one another for a year and then another. The young man continued growing up and even began to have a bit of the swagger of a New York bachelor, and he realized that to truly become a man, to truly become himself, he had to meet the person who had so shaped him through his correspondence. So, he wrote again, asking if in the event he came to St. Petersburg, he'd be able to visit the old master. The elder rabbi replied positively. Of course he could.

So, the young man packed his luggage and bought a ticket for a boat across the Atlantic. First England, then mainland Europe, then finally to St. Petersburg, the gilded city of Russia. Walking through the streets, carrying his teacher's address, he happened upon a market, and in the market, he happened upon a *matryoshka* doll. Looking up from the doll, he realized he was at his master's address. Soon he was up the five flights of stairs. He came to an ancient wooden door. He knocked. A voice called from the other side, saying he should come in.

He entered into a simple room. The floors were wood, and there was a neatly made bed, a few stacks of books, and a desk at which an old man, dressed in black, was writing. The young New Yorker was struck by the bareness of the room. Surely a teacher of such stature could afford a nice thing or two. But swallowing the thought, he said hello, nearly prostrating himself before the teacher. They spoke of the younger man's journey, the older man's scholarship, their mutual reverence to God. But then, as the conversation developed, the young man couldn't help himself.

"Where are your things?" the young man asked.

The master paused, looked at the young man's luggage, and replied.

"Well, where are yours?" the master asked.

"I'm just passing through," the young man answered.

Then the elder said, "So am I."

ACKNOWLEDGMENTS

NOBODY SUCCEEDS IN A SILO. The majority of our life's travels include a partner or two or many. Be it a significant other, friend, or business colleague, we most likely have some company. If I've learned anything from my life's journey, it's that our choice of partners—be it a life partner, cofounder, team member, or investor—can make or break a venture.

I believe the people we meet along the way are the people we are destined to meet. Positive or negative, they all play some kind of role.

The journey that became this book started many years back. The full set of people I need to thank will not fit on a few pages. My greatest thanks go to the universe for unveiling the people and the experiences that motivated me to take on this project.

My life would be completely lost if it wasn't for my family and friends. They carry me through every day. I am fortunate to have a life partner and a son who are the greatest sources of my inspiration.

I wish to especially thank our publishing and editorial team at Greenleaf and Fast Company Press for their professionalism and attention to this project. There are not enough words to describe my appreciation for my friend and publicist, who has been instrumental in moving me forward every day.

It is only when the right person shows up that we get to see why it has never worked the same way with anyone else. The connection, talent, enlightenment, and friendship I found in my coauthor are the only reason I am able to put out this book.

Thank you.

Faisal Hoque

———

I have always loved books and always longed for—and feared—the opportunity to write one. I have been especially enamored with these sweet little back pages, acknowledgments, liner notes, and the like. They show us another side of the writer and, in so doing, bring us closer to the author.

I am astounded that I have the opportunity to write such a note, to acknowledge the people who have helped me along the way.

Near the beginning of this year, I met a wise soul beneath the stars of Grand Central Station. We talked of Zen and entrepreneurship, poetry and products, life and life's work. I knew immediately that this person would become a part of my life's work. Thank you, Faisal, for inviting me on this epic adventure. I know it is the first of many.

I would also like to thank my mother, Nicole, my father, Robert, and my stepfather, David. As I grow older, I find myself saying things and acting just as they did. And I am fortunate to have such an inheritance of a love of learning and life. My dear siblings—Liza and Grant—are my anchors. I am honored to share this journey with them.

To list all the friends who are present in this book would be impossible, but I'll name a few: Ellie, Dan, Dana, Chloe, Johan, Matthias, Erik, Tim, Mark, Ted, Mike, Dan, John, Marianna, Katie, Ryan, Christina, Benjamin, Kevin, Jack, and Nilofer. You are all present here.

I must make a nod to my editors at Fast Company, who took me in as a stray and reared my writerly soul: Erin, Mac, Anjali, Tyler, and Noah. Thank you.

But a writer is nothing without a reader.

So, most of all, thank you.

Drake Baer

NOTES

Introduction

1. Drake Baer, "Evernote's Quest to Become a 100-Year Startup," *Fast Company*, June 13, 2013, http://www.fastcompany.com/3012870/dialed /evernotes-quest-to-become-a-100-year-old-startup.

Author's Note

1. Cynthia Cox, Rachel Garfield, Rabah Kamal and Nirmata Panchal, "The Implications of COVID-19 for Mental Health and Substance Abuse," *KFF*, February 10, 2021, https://www.kff.org/coronavirus-covid-19/issue-brief /the-implications-of-covid-19-for-mental-health-and-substance-use/.

2. Sarah Perez, "Meditation and Mindfulness Apps Continue Their Surge amid Pandemic," *TechCrunch*, May 28, 2020, https://techcrunch .com/2020/05/28/meditation-and-mindfulness-apps-continue-their -surge-amid-pandemic/.

Chapter 1

1. William Harris, *Heraclitus: The Complete Fragments*, http://community .middlebury.edu/~harris/Philosophy/heraclitus.pdf.

2. Shunryu Suzuki, *Zen Mind, Beginner's Mind* (Boston: Shambhala Publications, 2006), 77–81.

3. Nassim Taleb, *The Black Swan: The Impact of the Highly Improbable* (New York: Random House, 2010), 324–325. Also, his entire *Antifragile: Things That Gain from Disorder* (New York: Random House, 2012).

4. Thomas K. McCraw, *Prophet of Innovation: Joseph Schumpeter and Creative Destruction* (Boston: Harvard University Press, 2007).

5. Vijay Govindarajan and Chris Trimble, *Reverse Innovation: Create Far from Home, Win Everywhere* (Boston: Harvard Business Review Press, 2007).

6. Joseph Schumpeter, *Capitalism, Socialism and Democracy* (Harper & Brothers, 1942).

7. James N. Baron and Michael T. Hannan, "Organizational Blueprints for Success in High-Tech Start-Ups: Lessons from the Stanford Project on Emerging Companies," *California Management Review* 44, no. 3 (2002): 8–36.

8. Per email from Baron to Faisal and Drake, 2013.

9. Alfred Rappaport, *Saving Capitalism from Short-Termism: How to Build Long-Term Value and Take Back Our Financial Future* (New York: McGraw-Hill, 2012).

10. Clayton M. Christensen, *The Innovator's Dilemma* (New York: HarperBusiness, 2007).

11. Chuck Salter, "A Prescription for Innovation," *Fast Company*, April 1, 2006, http://www.fastcompany.com/56032/prescription-innovation.

12. Drake Baer, "Kickstarting: Molly Crabapple Versus the Establishment," *Fast Company*, April 12, 2013, http://www.fastcocreate.com/1682783 /kickstarting-molly-crabapple-versus-the-establishment.

13. Molly Crabapple, Interview.

14. Jack Dorsey, "The Innovator: Jack Dorsey," Interview by Lara Logan, *60 Minutes*, CBSNewsOnline, Video, http://www.youtube.com/watch ?feature=player_embedded&v=eKHoTOYTFH8.

Chapter 2

1. Katherine Tinsley, "The 35 Best Betty White Quotes in Honor of What Would've Been Her 100th Birthday," *Good Housekeeping*, January 17, 2022, https://www.goodhousekeeping.com/life/entertainment/a38768588/betty -white-quotes/.

2. Paul Slakey, Interview.

3. Scott R. Bishop, "Mindfulness: A Proposed Operational Definition," *Clinical Psychology: Science and Practice* 11, no. 3 (2004): 230–241.

4. Britta K. Hölzel, Sara W. Lazar, Tim Gard, Vev Schuman-Olivier, David R. Vago, and Ulrich Ott, "How Does Mindfulness Meditation Work? Proposing Mechanisms of Action from a Conceptual and Neural Perspective," *Perspectives on Psychological Science* 6, no. 537 (2011): 537–559.

5. Fadel Zeidana, Susan K. Johnson, Bruce J. Diamond, Zhanna David, and Paula Goolkasian, "Mindfulness Meditation Improves Cognition: Evidence of Brief Mental Training," *Consciousness and Cognition* (2009): 597–605.

6. "Mindfulness Meditation Training Changes Brain Structure in Eight Weeks," *Science Daily,* January 21, 2011, http://www.sciencedaily.com /releases/2011/01/110121144007.htm.

7. Scott R. Bishop, "Mindfulness: A Proposed Operational Definition," *Clinical Psychology: Science and Practice* 11, no. 3 (2004): 230–241.

8. Liz Kulze, "How Meditation Works," *The Atlantic*, June 27, 2013, https ://www.theatlantic.com/health/archive/2013/06/how-meditation-works /277275/.

9. Pema Chödrön, *Start Where You Are: A Guide to Compassionate Living* (Boston: Shambhala Publications, 2004).

10. Bhikkhu Bodhi, *The Noble Eightfold Path: Way to End Suffering* (Onalaska, WA: Pariyatti Publishing, 2006).

11. Bhante Y. Wimala, *Lessons of the Lotus: Practical Teachings of a Traveling Buddhist Monk* (New York: Bantam, 1997).

12. Joseph Campbell with Bill Moyers, *The Power of Myth* (New York: Anchor Books, 1991).

13. Richard Nisbett, *The Geography of Thought: How Asians and Westerners Think Differently . . . and Why* (New York: Free Press, 2004).

14. David Whyte, *Crossing the Unknown Sea: Work as a Pilgrimage of Identity* (New York: Riverhead Books, 2001).

15. Michael Schrage, *Who Do You Want Your Customers to Become?* (Boston: Harvard Business Review Press, 2012).

16. Steven Pressfield, *The War of Art: Break Through the Blocks and Win Your Inner Creative Battles* (New York: Black Irish Entertainment LLC, 2012).

17. Friedrich Nietzsche, *Basic Writings of Nietzsche* (New York: Modern Library, 2000).

18. Mihaly Csikszentmihalyi, *Flow: The Psychology of Optimal Experience* (New York: Harper Perennial, 2008).

19. Ron Adner, *The Wide Lens: A New Strategy for Innovation* (New York: Portfolio, 2012).

Chapter 3

1. Anaïs Nin, *The Diary of Anaïs Nin, Vol. 1: 1931–1934* (New York: Harcourt Inc., 1966).

2. Coleman Barks and Jalaluddin Rumi, *Rumi: The Book of Love: Poems of Ecstasy and Longing* (San Francisco: HarperOne, 2003).

3. "Trust Is the Lubricant for Transactions," Greystone Global, June 13, 2021, https://greystoneglobal.com/trust-is-the-lubricant-for-transactions/.

4. Aristotle, W. D. Ross, and Lesley Brown, *The Nicomachean Ethics* (Oxford: Oxford University Press, 2009).

5. Towers Watson, "Engagement at Risk: Driving Strong Performance in a Volatile Global Environment," 2012, https://employeeengagement.com /wp-content/uploads/2012/11/2012-Towers-Watson-Global-Workforce -Study.pdf.

6. McKinsey & Company, "The State of Human Capital 2012: False Summit," 2012, https://www.mckinsey.com/~/media/mckinsey/dotcom /client_service/organization/pdfs/state_of_human_capital_2012.ashx.

7. Drake Baer, "How to Know If You're Working with Mammals or Reptiles (and Why It Matters to Your Creativity)," *FastCoCreate*, February 7, 2013, Accessed April 24, 2013, http://www.fastcocreate.com/1682363/how-to -know-if-youre-working-with-mammals-or-reptiles-and-why-it-matters-to -your-creativity.

8. Henri Bergson, *The Creative Mind: An Introduction to Metaphysics* (Mineola, NY: Dover, 2010).

9. Robert C. Pozen, "They Work Long Hours, but What About Results?," *New York Times*, October 7, 2012, Accessed April 24, 2013, nytimes.com/2012 /10/07/business/measure-results-not-hours-to-improve-work-efficiency.html.

10. Anaïs Nin, *The Diary of Anaïs Nin, Vol. 1: 1931–1934* (New York: Harcourt Inc., 1966).

11. Drake Baer, "Bob Pozen, Master of Extreme Productivity, Shares His 3 Most Effective Career Tips." *Fast Company*, October 25, 2012, Accessed April 24, 2013, http://www.fastcompany.com/3002413/bob-pozen-master -extreme-productivity-shares-his-3-most-effective-career-tips.

12. Jeffrey Phillips, Ovo Innovations, "Too Busy to Innovate," March 21, 2013, Accessed April 24, 2013, http://innovateonpurpose.blogspot.com/2013/03 /too-busy-to-innovate.html.

13. Drake Baer, "Steelcase's Anthropologist on Remaking Offices to Create Happier Workers," *Fast Company*, January 3, 2013, Accessed April 24, 2013, http://www.fastcompany.com/3004140/steelcases-anthropologist -remaking-offices-create-happier-workers.

14. Dan Hill, "Knockabout Space," *Medium,* March 8, 2013, Accessed April 24, 2013, https://medium.com/on-management/b52aaa166a11.

15. Drake Baer, "Slacking at Work Is a Controversial Productivity Tool—So Is There a Better Way?," *Fast Company*, February 20, 2013, Accessed April 24, 2013, http://www.fastcompany.com/3006051/slacking-work-controversial -productivity-tool-so-there-better-way.

16. William Strunk and E. B. White, *The Elements of Style*, 4th ed. (New York: Longman, 2000).

Chapter 4

1. Lao-Tzu and Stephen Mitchell (trans.), *The Enlightened Heart: An Anthology of Sacred Poetry* (New York: Harper Perennial, 2011), 14.

2. Jonah Lehrer, "*Don't!* The Secret of Self-Control," *The New Yorker*, May 18, 2009, Accessed April 24, 2013, http://www.newyorker.com/reporting /2009/05/18/090518fa_fact_lehrer?currentPage=all.

3. "Value Creation: The Ultimate Measure by Which a Company Is Judged," *The Economist*, November 20, 2009, Accessed April 24, 2013, http://www .economist.com/node/14301714.

4. Carmen Nobel, "Clay Christensen's Milkshake Marketing," *HBS Working Knowledge*, February 14, 2011, http://hbswk.hbs.edu/item/6496.html.

5. Albert Camus, *The Myth of Sisyphus: And Other Essays* (New York: Vintage, 1991).

6. Jim Morrison and the Doors, "Five to One," *Waiting for the Sun,* 1968.

7. Geshe Ngawang Dhargyey, "Death and the Way," *Foundation for the Preservation of the Mahayana Tradition*, September 21, 2012, Accessed April 24, 2013, http://www.lamayeshe.com/?sect=article&id=378.

8. Jeff Bezos, Amazon.com, "Letter to Shareholders." April 2013, Accessed April 24, 2013, http://www.sec.gov/Archives/edgar/data/1018724 /000119312513151836/d511111dex991.htm.

9. Tim Carmody, "Surprise! Jeff Bezos Explains to Amazon Investors Why No Profits Are a Good Thing," *The Verge,* April 12, 2013, https://www.theverge .com/2013/4/12/4217794/jeff-bezos-letter-amazon-investors-2012.

10. Ellen McGirt, "How Nike's CEO Shook Up the Shoe Industry," *Fast Company*, September 1, 2010, Accessed April 24, 2013, http://www .fastcompany.com/1676902/how-nikes-ceo-shook-shoe-industry.

11. Nike Inc., "About Nike, Inc.," Accessed April 24, 2013, http://nikeinc .com/pages/about-nike-inc.

12. IKEA, "A Better Everyday Life," Accessed April 24, 2013, http://www.ikea .com/ms/en_US/about_ikea/the_ikea_way/our_business_idea/a_better _everyday_life.html.

13. Lauren Collins, "House Perfect," *The New Yorker*, September 26, 2011, https://www.newyorker.com/magazine/2011/10/03/house-perfect.

14. Simon Neville, "IKEA Profits up 8% in 2012," *The Guardian*, January 23, 2013, Accessed April 24, 2013, http://www.guardian.co.uk/business/2013 /jan/23/ikea-profits-rise-2012.

15. Annie Murphy Paul, "Annie Murphy Paul: Author-Journalist-Consultant-Speaker," Accessed April 24, 2013, http://anniemurphypaul.com/.

16. Donald L. Laurie, Yves L. Doz, and Claude L. Sheer, "Creating New Growth Platforms," *Harvard Business Review,* May, 2006, https://hbr.org /2006/05/creating-new-growth-platforms.

17. Leonard E. Read, Library of Economics and Liberty, "I, Pencil," 2000, Accessed April 24, 2013, https://www.econlib.org/library/Essays/rdPncl .html.

18. Kevin Ashton, "What Coke Contains," *Medium*, February 27, 2013, Accessed April 24, 2013, https://medium.com/@kevin_ashton/what-coke -contains-221d449929ef.

19. Brian Hurley, "Enabling the Creative Entrepreneur: Business Ecosystems," *Technology Innovation Management Review*, August 2009, https://timreview.ca/article/276.

Chapter 5

1. John Donne, "*The Works of John Donne*, vol 3 (London: John Parker, 1839).

2. Lauren A. Rivera, "Hiring as Cultural Matching: The Case of Elite Professional Service Firms," *American Sociological Review*, 2012, Accessed June 14, 2013, http://www.asanet.org/journals/ASR/Dec12ASRFeature.pdf.

3. Drake Baer, "Hiring, Like Dating, Sucks; Here's How Startups Are Trying to Fix It," *Fast Company*, February 28, 2013, Accessed June 14, 2013, http://www.fastcompany.com/3006365/hiring-dating-sucks-heres-how-startups-are-trying-fix-it.

4. Warren Buffett, "Warren Buffett Is Bullish . . . on Women," *Fortune*, May 22, 2013, Accessed June 13, 2013, https://www.cnn.com/2013/05/02/us/warren-buffett-is-bullish-on-women/index.html.

5. Melvin Conway, "How Do Committees Invent?," *Home Page of Melvin Conway*, Accessed June 10, 2013, http://www.melconway.com/research/committees.html.

6. Drake Baer, "How Yammer Makes Itself Disruption-Proof," *Fast Company*, June 28, 2013, http://www.fastcompany.com/3013548/dialed/how-yammer-makes-itself-disruption-proof.

7. Drake Baer, "Harvard Professor Finds That Innovative Ideas Spread Like the Flu; Here's How to Catch Them," *Fast Company*, http://www.fastcompany.com/3004829/harvard-professor-finds-innovative-ideas-spread-flu-heres-how-catch-them.

8. Noel Tichy, "Lafley's Legacy: From Crisis to Consumer-Driven," Bloomberg, June 10, 2009, Accessed June 11, 2013, https://www.bloomberg.com/news/articles/2009-06-10/lafleys-legacy-from-crisis-to-consumer-driven.

9. A. G. Lafley and Ram Charan, *The Game-Changer: How You Can Drive Revenue and Profit Growth with Innovation* (New York: Crown Business, 2008).

10. Hal Gregersen and Jeff Dyer, "How Procter & Gamble Keeps Its Innovation Edge," *Forbes*, April 12, 2012, http://www.forbes.com/sites/innovatorsdna /2012/04/12/how-procter-gamble-keeps-its-innovation-edge/.

11. Christina Bielaszka-DuVernay, "Broadening the Brand," *Harvard Business Review*, January 14, 2009, http://blogs.hbr.org/hmu/2009/01/broadening -the-brand.html.

12. Dave Gray and Thomas Vander Wal, *The Connected Company* (Sebastopol, CA: O'Reilly Media, 2012).

Chapter 6

1. Philip Hernandez, "What Meryl Streep Says About Acting," September 13, 2016, https://www.backstage.com/magazine/article/meryl-streep-says -acting-5578/.

2. Patrick Radden Keefe, "Spitballing Indy," *The New Yorker*, March 26, 2013, http://www.newyorker.com/online/blogs/culture/2013/03/spitballing-indy .html.

3. Judith Butler, "Gender Performativity," *Big Think*, December 10, 2011, Accessed June 18, 2013, http://www.youtube.com/watch?v=fndkPPJBi1U.

4. William Shakespeare and Horace H. Furness, *As You Like It* (New York: Dover Publications, 1963).

5. Tom Kelley and Jonathan Littman, *The Ten Faces of Innovation: IDEO's Strategies for Defeating the Devil's Advocate and Driving Creativity Throughout Your Organization* (New York: Doubleday, 2005).

6. Lou Adler, "There Are Only Four Jobs in the Whole World—Are You in the Right One?," *LinkedIn*, May 2, 2013, Accessed August 6, 2013, https://www.linkedin.com/pulse/20130502173937-15454-there-are -only-four-jobs-in-the-whole-world-are-you-in-the-right-one/.

7. Jennifer Rooney, "Behind The Scenes of Oreo's Real-Time Super Bowl Slam Dunk," *Forbes*, February 4, 2013, Accessed August 6, 2013, http://www .forbes.com/sites/jenniferrooney/2013/02/04/behind-the-scenes-of-oreos -real-time-super-bowl-slam-dunk/.

8. Charles Darwin and Leonard Kebler, *On the origin of species by means of natural selection, or, The preservation of favoured races in the struggle for life* (London: J. Murray, 1859).

9. Leigh Thompson, *Creative Conspiracy: The New Rules of Breakthrough Collaboration* (Boston: Harvard Business Review Press, 2013).

10. Martin Perlich, *The Art of the Interview: A Guide to Insightful Interviewing* (Los Angeles: Silman-James Press, 2007).

11. Barbara Fredrickson, "The Value of Positive Emotions," *American Scientist*, 2003, Accessed August 6, 2013, https://www.americanscientist.org/sites /americanscientist.org/files/20058214332_306.pdf.

12. Fredrickson, "The Value of Positive Emotions."

13. Barbara Fredrickson, Interview.

Chapter 7

1. Pema Chödrön, *Start Where You Are: A Guide to Compassionate Living* (Boston: Shambhala Publications, 2004).

2. Daniel H. Pink, *Drive: The Surprising Truth About What Motivates Us* (New York: Riverhead Books, 2011).

3. Bryan Buckhart, "Getting New Employees Off to a Good Start," *New York Times: You're The Boss*, March 13, 2013, http://boss.blogs.nytimes.com /2013/03/13/getting-employees-off-to-a-good-start/.

4. Drake Baer, "GitHub's Code for Workplace Happiness," *Fast Company*, April 26, 2013, http://www.fastcompany.com/3008758/githubs-code -workplace-happiness.

5. Belinda Luscombe, "Do We Need $75,000 a Year to Be Happy?," *Time*, September 6, 2010, https://content.time.com/time/magazine /article/0,9171,2019628,00.html.

6. Tom Stafford, "Why Money Can't Buy You Happiness," *BBC FUTURE*, March 27, 2013, http://www.bbc.com/future/story/20130326-why-money -cant-buy-you-happiness/1.

7. Reid Hoffman, Ben Casnocha, and Chris Yeh, "Tours of Duty: The New Employer-Employee Compact," *Harvard Business Review*, June 2013, http://hbr.org/2013/06/tours-of-duty-the-new-employer-employee -compact/ar/2.

8. Nihal Mehta, Interview.

9. Mortimer J. Adler and Charles Van Doren, *How to Read a Book: The Classic Guide to Intelligent Reading* (New York: Touchstone, 1972).

10. Teresa M. Amabile and Steven J. Kramer, "The Power of Small Wins," *Harvard Business Review*, May 2011, Accessed August 6, 2013, http://hbr .org/2011/05/the-power-of-small-wins/.

11. Walter Chen, Interview.

Chapter 8

1. Charles Baudelaire, "Correspondences," 1857, http://www.doctorhugo.org/ synaesthesia/baudelaire.html.

2. Nassim Taleb, *Antifragile: Things That Gain from Disorder* (New York: Random House, 2012).

3. Burkhard Bilger, "The Possibilian," *The New Yorker*, April 25, 2011, http:// www.newyorker.com/reporting/2011/04/25/110425fa_fact_bilger?current Page=all.

4. Serge Bramly, *Leonardo* (London: Penguin Books, 1994).

5. Philip Butta, "How Alcoa, Starbucks, Arista, and Febreze Kicked Normal Habits and Found Success," *Fast Company*, February 13, 2012, http://www .fastcompany.com/1812065/how-alcoa-starbucks-arista-and-febreze-kicked -normal-habits-and-found-success.

6. Edward Nęcka and Teresa Hlawacz, "Who Has an Artistic Temperament? Relationships Between Creativity and Temperament Among Artists and Bank Officers," *Creativity Research Journal* 25, no. 2 (2013), http://www .tandfonline.com/doi/abs/10.1080/10400419.2013.783744.

7. Scott Barry Kaufman, "How Do Artists Differ from Bank Officers?," *Scientific American*, June 15, 2013, http://blogs.scientificamerican.com /beautiful-minds/2013/06/15/how-do-artists-differ-from-bank-officers/.

8. Edward Nęcka and Teresa Hlawacz, "Who Has an Artistic Temperament? Relationships Between Creativity and Temperament Among Artists and Bank Officers," *Creativity Research Journal* 25, no. 2 (2013), http://www .tandfonline.com/doi/abs/10.1080/10400419.2013.783744.

9. Emilie Baltz, Interview.

10. Drake Baer, "Google Ventures' Secret Mantra for Super-Productive Meetings," *Fast Company*, March 25, 2013, https://www.fastcompany .com/3007363/google-ventures-secret-mantra-super-productive-meetings.

Chapter 9

1. William Strunk and E. B. White, *The Elements of Style*, 4th ed. (New York: Longman, 2000).

2. Tom Gardner, "A Foolish Interview with Michael Mauboussin," *Motley Fool*, September 12, 2012, http://www.fool.com/investing/beginning /2012/09/19/a-foolish-interview-with-michael-mauboussin.aspx.

3. Drake Baer, "Email Is a Universal Plague; Can Mailbox Make It Manageable Again?," *Fast Company*, February 7, 2013, Accessed August 6, 2013, http://www.fastcompany.com/3005538/email-universal-plague-can -mailbox-make-it-manageable-again.

4. Gentry Underwood, Interview.

5. Alexia Tsotsis and Leena Rao, "Mailbox Cost Dropbox Around $100 Million," *Techcrunch* (blog), March 15, 2013, http://techcrunch.com /2013/03/15/mailbox-cost-dropbox-around-100-million/.

6. Serge Bramly, *Leonardo* (London: Penguin Books, 1994).

Chapter 10

1. Stephen Levy, "Jeff Bezos Owns the Web in More Ways Than You Think," *Wired*, December 13, 2011, http://www.wired.com/magazine/2011/11 /ff_bezos/all/1.

2. Carmine Gallo, "How Apple Store Seduces You with the Tilt of Its Laptops," *Forbes*, June 14, 2012, http://www.forbes.com/sites/carminegallo /2012/06/14/why-the-new-macbook-pro-is-tilted-70-degrees-in-an-apple -store/.

3. Bing Gordon, Interview, May 9, 2013.

4. Richard L. Evans, *Richard Evans' Quote Book* (Salt Lake City: Publishers Press, 1971).

5. Serge Bramly, *Leonardo* (London: Penguin Books, 1994).

Chapter 11

1. Jack Steward, "The Ultimate List of Remote Work Statistics for 2022," *Findstack*, February 3, 2022, https://findstack.com/remote-work-statistics/.

2. Katherine Schaeffer, "U.S. Has Changed in Key Ways in the Past Decade, from Tech Use to Demographics," *Pew Research Center,* December 20, 2019, https://www.pewresearch.org/fact-tank/2019/12/20/key-ways-us -changed-in-past-decade/.

3. Tim Minahan, "What Your Future Employees Want Most," *Harvard Business Review*, May 31, 2021, https://hbr.org/2021/05/what-your-future -employees-want-most.

4. Bjornsjo Agneta, Kevin Quiring, and Bill Theofilou, "Life Reimagined— Mapping the Motivations That Matter for Today's Consumers," *Accenture*, 2021, https://www.accenture.com/bg-en/insights/strategy/_acnmedia /Thought-Leadership-Assets/PDF-5/Accenture-Life-Reimagined-Full -Report.pdf.

5. Andre Terzic and Scott Waldman, "Health Care Evolves from Reactive to Proactive," *U.S. National Library of Medicine*, December 29, 2018, https ://ascpt.onlinelibrary.wiley.com/doi/10.1002/cpt.1295.

Chapter 12

1. Bill George, "Mindfulness Is Transforming Leadership," *The Huffington Post*, November 11, 2015, https://www.huffpost.com/entry/mindfulness-is -transformi_b_8539894.

2. D. M. Davis and J. A. Hayes, "What Are the Benefits of Mindfulness? A Practice Review of Psychotherapy-Related Research," *APA Psychotherapy*, 2011, https://www.apa.org/pubs/journals/features/pst-48-2-198.pdf.

Chapter 13

1. Courtney Ackerman, "What Is Resilience and Why Is It So Important to Bounce Back?," *Positive Psychology*, July 12, 2021, https://positive psychology.com/what-is-resilience/.

2. Faisal Hoque, *Survive to Thrive* (Motivational Press, 2014).

RECOMMENDED READING

AS AUTHORS, WE HAVE the privilege of standing on the shoulders of giants. As authors of a holistic business book, these giants come from diverse backgrounds. To that point, if you'd like to further explore the intersections of mindfulness and innovation mapped out in this book, please open up these titles.

ON MEDITATION

The Miracle of Mindfulness **by Thich Nhat Hanh**

When people ask us about meditation, this is the first book we recommend. If you don't yet know him, Nhat Hanh was a Vietnamese Zen Master and one of the foremost living Buddhist teachers. This slim book, now a classic, took shape from a series of letters to a friend about the nature of meditation. It serves as the most lucid introduction to the practice.

Start Where You Are **by Pema Chödrön**

If *Miracle* is a perfect introduction to mindfulness, *Start Where You Are* is the perfect introduction to loving-kindness meditation. Structured around a centuries-old Tibetan Buddhist of arising compassion, this American nun's pragmatic approach to the problem (and opportunity) of suffering is something you will find yourself walking around with, whether or not the book is in your hand.

ON HUMAN EXPERIENCE

Flow by Mihaly Csikszentmihalyi

In *Flow*, Csikszentmihalyi, a Hungarian-American psychologist, advances the argument that your life is the product of the way you invest your attention. That attention is best invested in a state of flow. It's that sweet spot where your skills match the challenge at hand, whether it's playing tennis, managing a company, or writing a book. And like a good teacher, Csikszentmihalyi helps us to see how to structure more flow into our lives.

The Power of Myth by Joseph Campbell

When we talk about myth, we tend to marginalize the word. To mythologize is to make grand, yes, but also to make unreal and unrelatable. Campbell, the comparative mythologist and student of Carl Jung, spent a lifetime explaining how the mythic may be the most real thing we have— for myths are simply how we organize meaning in our lives. *The Power of Myth* comes from a series of interviews he did with Bill Moyers at the conclusion of his career. By the end, we see the way Campbell structured meaning in his life.

ON PEOPLE AT WORK

Give and Take by Adam Grant

What if the people that get ahead are those who give the most? Such is the argument of Wharton organizational psychologist Adam Grant. He divides the working world into takers (people who are always looking to extract value), matchers (people who are always looking for an even split), and givers (people who are always looking to help). Intriguingly enough, it's the givers who get the most in the end.

The Progress Principle by Teresa Amabile

How do we ensure people find themselves doing meaningful work? What's the connection between meaning and engagement? How does all this relate to innovation and financial success? In *The Progress Principle*, Harvard Business School research director Teresa Amabile makes clear the implicit, often murky qualities of our interior lives at work. With that helpful articulation, we can work a little—or a lot—better.

ON INNOVATION

The Innovator's Dilemma by Clayton Christensen

The original and still the best, Christensen's *Dilemma* dissects our innovation economy and helps us see why creativity presents such a dilemma to organizations as they grow. Few books of the past thirty years have had such an influence on business and provided a vocabulary for the way we work. For these reasons and more, this is a must read.

The Lean Startup by Eric Ries

The thing about people is they don't really know what they want—but innovators can provide it for them. In *The Lean Startup*, entrepreneur-turned-guru Eric Ries provides a roadmap for rapidly bringing products to market and allowing the customer to tell you if you're making what they need. Ries' work has become orthodoxy in the startup world, so we'd do well to know it. (How else can we rebel?)

ON WHERE WE ARE NOW

The Connected Company by Dave Gray with Thomas Vander Wal

The walls that separate company from customer are growing ever more porous. *The Connected Company* shows how, exactly, this is happening, and what it means for the structures and running of our organizations. Plus, it has terrific illustrations—always a bonus.

11 Rules for Creating Value in the Social Era by Nilofer Merchant

Our friend Nilofer Merchant has surveyed the newly forming geography of the working world. In this book, we come realize how much the *Social Era* is about much more than social media. More than spending our days on Twitter and Facebook, we've now shifted paradigms into openness and fluidity. As such, organizations that were once gorillas need to turn into gazelles.

ON MANAGEMENT

The Essential Drucker by Peter Drucker

Few people embody a craft as Drucker embodied management. This book distills six decades of his insights into the philosophy of business. As such, it's required reading for anyone thinking deeply about the way we work.

ABOUT THE AUTHORS

Photo Credit: Michael Graham

FAISAL HOQUE is an accomplished entrepreneur; noted thought leader; technology innovator; advisor to CEOs, BODs, and the US federal government; and an author with more than twenty-five years of cross-industry success. He is the founder of Shadoka, NextChapter, and other companies. They focus on enabling sustainable and transformational changes. He is a three-time winning founder and CEO of Deloitte Technology Fast 50 and Deloitte Technology Fast 500 awards.

Throughout his career, he has developed over twenty commercial business and technology platforms and worked with public- and private-sector giants such as US Department of Defense (DoD), GE, MasterCard, American Express, Northrop Grumman, CACI, PepsiCo, IBM, Home Depot, Netscape, Infosys, French Social Security Services, Gartner, Cambridge Technology Partners, JP Morgan Chase, CSC, and others. What sets Faisal apart is the unique position and perspective he has always maintained, which is grounded in hardcore technology with deep roots in leading-edge management science.

As a thought leader, he has authored a number of books on leadership, innovation, mindfulness, resilience, organizational transformation, and entrepreneurship, including the #1 *Wall Street Journal* and *USA Today* bestseller *LIFT—Fostering the Leader in You Amid Revolutionary Global Change*. His work has appeared in *Fast Company, Business Insider, Wall Street Journal, Businessweek, Fox, CBS, Financial Times, Mergers & Acquisitions, Forbes, Leadership Excellence*, and the *Huffington Post*, among other publications.

American Management Association (AMA) named him one of the Leaders to Watch. The editors of Ziff-Davis Enterprise named him one of the Top 100 Most Influential People in Technology alongside leading entrepreneurs such as Steve Jobs, Bill Gates, Michael Dell, Larry Page, and others. Trust Across America-Trust Around the World (TAA-TWA) named him one of the Top 100 Thought Leaders alongside global leaders such as Bill George, Doug Conant, Howard Schultz, and others.

His book *The Power of Convergence* (published by the American Management Association) was released in April 2011 and almost immediately was named One of the Best Business Books of 2011 by 800CEOREAD and CIO Insight. Two of his previous books, *Sustained Innovation* and *Winning the 3-Legged Race*, were also included in the Top 5 Transformation Books of the last few years, while *Sustained Innovation* also ranked in *CIO Insight Magazine*'s Editor's Picks: The 10 Best Business Books of 2007.

His broad areas of expertise include innovation, leadership, management, sustainable growth, transformation, strategy, governance, M&A, frameworks, and digital platforms.

He holds a strong belief that it is through knowledge sharing that we may provide the greatest clarity on how to improve our collective future. As a globetrotter, he is passionate about nature, people, culture, music, and design, and he loves to cook.

For more info, visit www.faisalhoque.com or follow him on Twitter @faisal_hoque and on LinkedIn: www.linkedin.com/in/faisalhoque/

Photo Credit: Drake Baer

DRAKE BAER is Insider's first editor at large, working across the newsroom to help produce ambitious journalism.

For two and a half years before that, Baer served as deputy editor, overseeing a team of twenty-plus reporters and editors who cover the future of work, real estate, and small business. The fast-paced team was behind some of Insider's major packages in the last few years, including a state-by-state look into unemployment during the first year of the pandemic and in-depth profiles of "niche famous" characters such as real estate media tycoon Brandon Turner and HR icon Johnny C. Taylor. They shed new light on big names, like Joe Biden, America's imperfect leader. He also cultivated thesis-oriented ideas journalism, whether it be on why "'diversity' and 'inclusion' are the emptiest words in corporate America" or why it's actually a horrible time to buy a house. (No, really, it is.)

Before editing, his byline as a reporter was on the masthead for *Fast Company* and *New York Magazine*, covering the many intersections of social science, business, and economics. Baer has interviewed some of our time's leading minds, including philanthropist Bill Gates, FiveThirtyEight founder Nate Silver, NBA champion and investor Steph Curry, "growth mindset" psychologist Carol Dweck, the rapper Q-Tip, Nobel laureate Daniel Kahneman, and the man who gave a name to "disruptive innovation," the late Clay Christensen.

Baer has published two books, the most recent being *Perception: How Our Bodies Shape Our Minds,* with Dennis Proffitt. He has been featured as a speaker at the Aspen Ideas Festival, presented at TedX Princeton, and moderated many panels.

Fun facts? He's meditated every day for over a decade, except for the days he hasn't. He circumnavigated the globe before turning twenty-five. He loves and can advocate for just about every food except grapefruit. And at thirty-five, he is just now learning to draw.